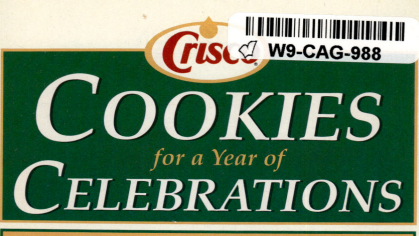

Crisco

COOKIES
for a Year of
CELEBRATIONS

Over 50 Great Cookies from 5 Easy Doughs

INTRODUCTION

Cookies have always been well liked, but every year their popularity seems to grow. Since they are quick to make and easy to transport, cookies fit so easily into today's casual lifestyle. They are as welcome in a child's lunch box as they are at a Fourth-of-July picnic.

Chocolate chip, oatmeal, peanut butter, brownie and sugar cookies are everyone's favorites. The Crisco Kitchens have developed five stellar recipes, one for each of these cookies. In addition to being delicious, these five cookies bake up high and stay soft, moist and chewy—just the way you like them. And these basic recipes are as versatile as they are delectable. Take any one of them, make a few changes and you have a new, exciting and sensational cookie. In fact, there is an entire chapter of great cookies that are easy variations of the basic recipe.

The secret to these moist and chewy cookies is Crisco, the country's leading all-vegetable shortening. Since Crisco never needs refrigeration, there is no need to allow it to soften. It is always ready when you are, so cookies made with Crisco can be baked on the spur of the moment. And now that Crisco Sticks are in supermarkets right next to the familiar blue cans of Crisco and the yellow cans of Butter Flavor Crisco, measuring is as easy as can be. Merely cut the pre-measured foil wrapper for the appropriate amount.

Home bakers can feel confident about using Crisco, since it contains half the saturated fat of butter. (Crisco contains 12 grams of total fat per tablespoon, of which 3 grams are saturated fat, while butter contains 7 grams of saturated fat per tablespoon.)

Some of the mouthwatering cookies on the following pages are pictured in specific holiday settings, but they are not exclusive to those times. While St. Pat's Pinwheels were developed to reflect the green theme of St. Patrick's Day, the peppermint–flavored swirl would be just as enjoyable at Christmas or at a graduation party. So use your imagination and enjoy these cookies all year round. Let the versatility of these five cookie recipes make any get-together a special occasion.

TIPS FOR BAKING GREAT COOKIES EVERY TIME

General Guidelines

• Read the entire recipe before you begin to make sure you have all the ingredients and baking utensils.

• Prepare baking pans and baking sheets according to recipe directions. Grease pans with Crisco only when greasing is called for in directions. Adjust oven racks and preheat the oven.

• Measure all ingredients accurately.

• Follow the recipe directions and baking times exactly. Check for doneness at the minimum baking time using the test given in the recipe.

Measuring

• Use standardized dry measuring cups for all dry ingredients and ingredients such as Crisco, peanut butter, nuts, dried fruit, coconut, fresh fruit, jams and jellies.

• Spoon flour into the correct measuring cup to overflowing and level it off with the straight edge of a metal spatula. Do not dip the measuring cup into the flour or tap the measuring cup on the counter as this will pack the flour.

• Press brown sugar into the correct measuring cup, fill to overflowing and level it off with a straight edge. It should hold the shape of the cup when turned out.

• Press Crisco or Butter Flavor Crisco into the correct measuring cup. Cut through with a knife or spatula and press again to eliminate air pockets. Level it off with a straight edge.

• Use standardized glass or clear plastic liquid measuring cups with a pouring spout to measure all liquid ingredients. Place the cup on a level surface, fill to the desired mark and check the measurement at eye level.

• Use standardized graduated measuring spoons, not eating or serving spoons, for measuring small amounts of ingredients. For dry ingredients, fill the spoon to overflowing and level it off with a straight edge.

Mixing

• Beat Crisco, sugar and other ingredients according to the recipe directions for several minutes to insure proper creaming.

• Sifting of flour is not necessary. Stir together the flour, baking soda, salt and spices before adding to the shortening mixture. Larger amounts of flour should be added gradually to the shortening mixture.

• Do not overmix the dough as this will toughen cookies. If using a hand mixer, it may be necessary to stir in the last portion of flour with a wooden spoon.

• Stir in chips, raisins, nuts and fruit with a wooden spoon.

Baking

• Use sturdy baking sheets with little or no sides. Allow 1 inch of space between the baking sheet and the sides of the oven. This allows heat to circulate in the oven during baking and promotes even browning. Cookies baked on insulated baking sheets may need 1 to 2 minutes longer baking time.

• Bake only one baking sheet at a time in the center of the oven. If cookies brown unevenly, rotate the baking sheet from front to back halfway through the baking time. If you do use more than one baking sheet at a time, rotate the sheets from the top rack to the bottom rack halfway through baking time. Space oven racks 6 inches apart. Allow the baking sheets to cool between batches. Dough will spread if placed on a hot baking sheet.

• Watch cookies carefully during baking to avoid overbaking. Follow the recipe for yield and size since baking time is determined for that size cookie.

• Allow cookies to remain on baking sheets for 2 minutes before removing to sheets of foil, unless otherwise stated. Cool cookies completely before storing.

Problem Solving

• Cookies are dry: This is usually the result of using too much flour or too little liquid. Always measure ingredients accurately.

• Cookies are too brown: If only the bottoms are too brown, the baking sheet may be too close to the bottom of the oven.

Move the rack to a higher position. If both the tops and bottoms of cookies are too brown, either the oven is too hot or there is insufficient air circulation around the baking sheet. Check the oven temperature with an oven thermometer or use a smaller baking sheet. Another cause of overbrowning is overbaking. Check cookies for doneness at the minimum baking time.

• Cookies spread too much or spread into each other: One of the most common causes for cookies spreading too much is using too little flour or too much liquid. Placing cookie dough on hot baking sheets or making cookies too large are other possible causes. Always cool baking sheets to room temperature before reusing and follow recipe directions and yield for proper-sized cookies. If cookies are the correct size but still spread into each other, the portioned dough may have been placed too close together on the baking sheet.

Storage

• Store cooled cookies at room temperature in airtight containers. Store each kind separately to prevent transfer of flavor and changes in texture. Freeze baked cookies in airtight containers or freezer bags for up to six months.

TIPS ON PACKING COOKIES FOR MAILING

• Wrap large, delicate or decorated cookies individually in plastic wrap. Pack cookies in an airtight container. Place heavier cookies at the bottom of the container or pack them in a separate container.

• Place the container in a larger box. Cushion with crumpled newspaper, styrofoam or air–popped popcorn. For a more festive look, wrap the container in gift paper and cushion with crumpled colored tissue paper or metallic tinsel.

• Bar cookies can be baked in disposable aluminum foil pans. When cool, cover pans with foil and pack the pans in a box. Cushion with crumpled newspaper.

• Seal outer box with packing tape.

ULTIMATE CHOCOLATE CHIP COOKIES

Luscious morsels of chocolate and perhaps some crunchy pecans nestled in a soft chewy cookie richly flavored with brown sugar and vanilla—these are the qualities you'll find in Crisco's Ultimate Chocolate Chip Cookies. And, as you will see on the pages that follow, this all-time family favorite recipe can be dressed up for special occasions and the familiar flavors of chocolate and pecans can be traded for a variety of different tastes.

This taste-tempting recipe can be easily varied to create cookies that bear no resemblance to a traditional chocolate chip cookie. Lemonade Cookies with their refreshing citrus flavor are just right for a bridal shower and Maple Walnut Cookies will become a much loved late-night snack. Captivate the kids with Peanut Butter Treats by simply substituting quartered miniature peanut butter cups for the chocolate chips and pecans.

In this chapter are ideas for festive Christmas cookies, such as Cherry Chocolate Chippies and Frosty's Colorful Cookies. Coffee Chip Drops are perfect for your Valentine's Day sweetheart and Pecan Pralines with bits of caramelized sugar and pecans are a perfect addition to any springtime celebration. Whatever variations you choose to bake, the results will delight everyone!

Ultimate Chocolate Chip Cookies
(page 8)

Ultimate Chocolate Chip Cookies

1¼ cups firmly packed light
    brown sugar
¾ cup Butter Flavor Crisco
    all-vegetable shortening
    or ¾ Butter Flavor
    Crisco Stick
2 tablespoons milk
1 tablespoon vanilla

1 egg
1¾ cups all-purpose flour
1 teaspoon salt
¾ teaspoon baking soda
1 cup (6 ounces) semisweet
    chocolate chips
1 cup coarsely chopped
    pecans* (optional)

*If pecans are omitted, add an additional ½ cup semisweet chocolate chips.

1. Heat oven to 375°F. Place sheets of foil on countertop for cooling cookies.

2. Place brown sugar, shortening, milk and vanilla in large bowl. Beat at medium speed of electric mixer until well blended. Add egg; beat well.

3. Combine flour, salt and baking soda. Add to shortening mixture; beat at low speed just until blended. Stir in chocolate chips and pecans, if desired.

4. Drop dough by rounded measuring tablespoonfuls 3 inches apart onto ungreased baking sheets.

5. Bake one baking sheet at a time at 375°F for 8 to 10 minutes for chewy cookies, or 11 to 13 minutes for crisp cookies. *Do not overbake.* Cool 2 minutes on baking sheet. Remove cookies to foil to cool completely. *Makes about 3 dozen cookies*

Pistachio and White Chocolate Cookies

1 cup shelled pistachio nuts
1¼ cups firmly packed light brown
    sugar
¾ cup Butter Flavor Crisco
    all-vegetable shortening or ¾
    Butter Flavor Crisco Stick
2 tablespoons milk
1 tablespoon vanilla
1 egg
1¾ cups all-purpose flour
1 teaspoon salt
¾ teaspoon baking soda
1 cup white chocolate chips or chunks

1. Heat oven to 350°F. Spread pistachio nuts on baking sheet. Bake at 350°F for 7 to 10 minutes or until toasted, stirring several times. Place nuts in kitchen towel; rub with towel to remove most of skin. Cool nuts. Chop coarsely; reserve.

2. *Increase oven temperature to 375°F.* Place sheets of foil on countertop for cooling cookies.

3. Place brown sugar, shortening, milk and vanilla in large bowl. Beat at medium speed of electric mixer until well blended. Add egg; beat well.

4. Combine flour, salt and baking soda. Add to shortening mixture; beat at low speed just until blended. Stir in white chocolate chips and reserved pistachios.

5. Drop dough by rounded measuring tablespoonfuls 3 inches apart onto ungreased baking sheets.

6. Bake one baking sheet at a time at 375°F for 8 to 10 minutes for chewy cookies, or 11 to 13 minutes for crisp cookies. *Do not overbake.* Cool 2 minutes on baking sheet. Remove cookies to foil to cool completely.
              Makes about 3 dozen cookies

For a festive Christmas buffet table, tie the silverware and napkins with brightly colored ribbons, tucking in sprigs of evergreen for an aromatic touch. Or try stuffing silverware into small, inexpensive stockings along with tiny gaily wrapped gifts for each guest.

Maple Walnut Cookies

1¼ cups firmly packed light brown sugar
¾ cup Butter Flavor Crisco all-vegetable shortening or ¾ Butter Flavor Crisco Stick
2 tablespoons maple syrup
1 teaspoon vanilla
1 teaspoon maple extract
1 egg
1¾ cups all-purpose flour
1 teaspoon salt
¾ teaspoon baking soda
½ teaspoon cinnamon
1½ cups chopped walnuts
30 to 40 walnut halves

1. Heat oven to 375°F. Place sheets of foil on countertop for cooling cookies.

2. Place brown sugar, shortening, maple syrup, vanilla and maple extract in large bowl. Beat at medium speed of electric mixer until well blended. Add egg; beat well.

3. Combine flour, salt, baking soda and cinnamon. Add to shortening mixture; beat at low speed just until blended. Stir in chopped walnuts.

4. Drop dough by rounded measuring tablespoonfuls 3 inches apart onto ungreased baking sheets. Press walnut half into center of each cookie.

5. Bake one baking sheet at a time at 375°F for 8 to 10 minutes for chewy cookies, or 11 to 13 minutes for crisp cookies. *Do not overbake.* Cool 2 minutes on baking sheet. Remove cookies to foil to cool completely.

Makes about 3 dozen cookies

Top to bottom: Maple Walnut Cookies, Peanut Butter Treats (page 21)

Lemonade Cookies

Need an idea for a party that will appeal to both children and adults? Plan an ice cream party—it's sure to please everyone. Set a buffet table with several flavors of ice cream or frozen yogurt, allowing at least two medium scoops per person. (One quart will yield about eight medium scoops of ice cream.) Provide a variety of sundae toppers — ice cream toppings, fruits, nuts and candies. Broken cookies such as Peanut Butter Treats (page 21) and Chewy Brownie Cookies (page 80) make great toppers. And be sure to include these citrus-flavored Lemonade Cookies as a delicious accompaniment.

1¼ cups granulated sugar
¾ cup Butter Flavor Crisco
    all-vegetable shortening
    or ¾ Butter Flavor Crisco Stick
2 tablespoons freshly squeezed lemon
    juice
1 tablespoon grated lemon peel
1 teaspoon vanilla
1 teaspoon lemon extract
1 egg
1¾ cups all-purpose flour
¾ teaspoon baking soda
½ teaspoon salt
½ cup flaked coconut (optional)

1. Heat oven to 375°F. Place sheets of foil on countertop for cooling cookies.

2. Place sugar, shortening, lemon juice, lemon peel, vanilla and lemon extract in large bowl. Beat at medium speed of electric mixer until well blended. Add egg; beat well.

3. Combine flour, baking soda and salt. Add to shortening mixture; beat at low speed just until blended.

4. Drop dough by rounded measuring tablespoonfuls 3 inches apart onto ungreased baking sheets. Sprinkle tops with coconut, if desired.

5. Bake one baking sheet at a time at 375°F for 8 to 10 minutes or until cookies are set and edges are lightly browned. (Watch closely; do not allow coconut to burn.) *Do not overbake.* Cool 2 minutes on baking sheet. Remove cookies to foil to cool completely.   *Makes about 3 dozen cookies*

Top to bottom: Chocolate Chip Ice Cream Sandwiches (page 14), Lemonade Cookies

Chocolate Chip Ice Cream Sandwiches

1¼ cups firmly packed light
    brown sugar
¾ cup Butter Flavor Crisco
    all-vegetable shortening
    or ¾ Butter Flavor
    Crisco Stick
2 tablespoons milk
1 tablespoon vanilla

1 egg
1¾ cups all-purpose flour
1 teaspoon salt
¾ teaspoon baking soda
1 cup semisweet chocolate
    chips
1 cup chopped pecans
2 pints ice cream, any flavor

1. Heat oven to 375°F. Place sheets of foil on countertop for cooling cookies.

2. Place brown sugar, shortening, milk and vanilla in large bowl. Beat at medium speed of electric mixer until well blended. Add egg; beat well.

3. Combine flour, salt and baking soda. Add to shortening mixture; beat at low speed just until blended. Stir in chocolate chips and pecans.

4. Measure ¼ cup dough; shape into ball. Repeat with remaining dough. Place balls 4 inches apart on ungreased baking sheets. Flatten balls into 3-inch circles.

5. Bake one baking sheet at a time at 375°F for 10 to 12 minutes or until cookies are lightly browned. *Do not overbake.* Cool 2 minutes on baking sheet. Remove cookies to foil to cool completely.

6. Remove ice cream from freezer to soften slightly. Measure ½ cup ice cream; spread onto bottom of one cookie. Cover with flat side of second cookie. Wrap sandwich in plastic wrap. Place in freezer. Repeat with remaining cookies and ice cream.

Makes about 10 ice cream sandwiches

Note: Chocolate Chip Ice Cream Sandwiches should be eaten within two days. After two days, cookies will absorb moisture and become soggy. If longer storage is needed, make and freeze cookies, but assemble ice cream sandwiches within two days of serving.

Mocha Chips 'n' Bits

Cookies

1¼ cups firmly packed light
   brown sugar
¾ cup Butter Flavor Crisco
   all-vegetable shortening
   or ¾ Butter Flavor
   Crisco Stick
2 tablespoons milk
1 tablespoon instant coffee
   powder
1 tablespoon vanilla
1 egg
1¾ cups all-purpose flour
1½ tablespoons unsweetened
   cocoa powder

1 teaspoon salt
¾ teaspoon baking soda
1 cup (6 ounces) milk
   chocolate chips
1 cup coarsely chopped
   pecans
4 ounces bittersweet
   chocolate, cut into
   chunks

Icing

1 cup white chocolate chips
1 teaspoon Crisco
   all-vegetable shortening

1. Heat oven to 375°F. Place sheets of foil on countertop for cooling cookies.

2. Place brown sugar, shortening, milk, instant coffee and vanilla in large bowl. Beat at medium speed of electric mixer until well blended. Add egg; beat well.

3. Combine flour, cocoa, salt and baking soda. Add to shortening mixture; beat at low speed just until blended. Stir in chocolate chips, pecans and chocolate chunks.

4. Drop dough by rounded measuring tablespoonfuls 3 inches apart onto ungreased baking sheets.

5. Bake one baking sheet at a time at 375°F for 8 to 10 minutes for chewy cookies, or 11 to 13 minutes for crisp cookies. *Do not overbake.* Cool 2 minutes on baking sheet. Remove cookies to foil to cool completely.

6. For icing, place white chocolate chips and shortening in heavy, resealable sandwich bag; seal bag. Microwave at 50% (MEDIUM) for 1 minute. Knead bag. If necessary, microwave at 50% for another 30 seconds at a time until mixture is smooth when kneaded. Cut small tip off corner of bag. Pipe shapes on cookies or drizzle randomly.

Makes about 3 dozen cookies

Note: White chocolate chips and shortening can be melted by placing resealable bag in bowl of hot water.

Chocolate Chip Cookie Bars

1¼ cups firmly packed light brown
    sugar
¾ cup Butter Flavor Crisco
    all-vegetable shortening or ¾
    Butter Flavor Crisco Stick
2 tablespoons milk
1 tablespoon vanilla
1 egg
1¾ cups all-purpose flour
1 teaspoon salt
¾ teaspoon baking soda
1 cup (6 ounces) semisweet chocolate
    chips
1 cup coarsely chopped pecans*
    (optional)

*If pecans are omitted, add an additional
½ cup semisweet chocolate chips.

1. Heat oven to 350°F. Grease 13 × 9-inch
baking pan. Place cooling rack on
countertop.

2. Place brown sugar, shortening, milk and
vanilla in large bowl. Beat at medium speed
of electric mixer until well blended. Add
egg; beat well.

3. Combine flour, salt and baking soda. Add
to shortening mixture; beat at low speed just
until blended. Stir in chocolate chips and
pecans, if desired.

4. Press dough evenly onto bottom of
prepared pan.

5. Bake at 350°F for 20 to 25 minutes or
until lightly browned and firm in the center.
Do not overbake. Cool completely on cooling
rack. Cut into 2 × 1½-inch bars.
                    Makes about 3 dozen bars

*Bar cookies are done
when the center is
firm to the touch or
a wooden pick
inserted in the
center comes out
clean.*

~

*The best way to store
bar cookies is right
in the pan in which
they were baked.
Cover tightly with
plastic wrap or
aluminum foil.*

Chocolate Chip Cookie Bars

Coffee Chip Drops

Chocolate kiss candies atop these coffee-flavored cookies send a loving message to your sweetheart on Valentine's Day.

1¼ cups firmly packed light brown
     sugar
¾ cup Butter Flavor Crisco
     all-vegetable shortening
     or ¾ Butter Flavor Crisco Stick
2 tablespoons cold coffee
1 teaspoon vanilla
1 egg
1¾ cups all-purpose flour
1 tablespoon finely ground French
     roast or espresso coffee beans
1 teaspoon salt
¾ teaspoon baking soda
½ cup semisweet chocolate chips
½ cup milk chocolate chips
½ cup coarsely chopped walnuts
30 to 40 chocolate kiss candies,
     unwrapped

1. Heat oven to 375°F. Place sheets of foil on countertop for cooling cookies.

2. Place brown sugar, shortening, coffee and vanilla in large bowl. Beat at medium speed of electric mixer until well blended. Add egg; beat well.

3. Combine flour, ground coffee, salt and baking soda. Add to shortening mixture; beat at low speed just until blended. Stir in chocolate chips and walnuts.

4. Drop dough by rounded measuring tablespoonfuls 2 inches apart onto ungreased baking sheets.

5. Bake one baking sheet at a time at 375°F for 8 to 10 minutes or until cookies are lightly browned and just set. *Do not overbake.* Place 1 candy in center of each cookie. Cool 2 minutes on baking sheet. Remove cookies to foil to cool completely.
Makes about 3 dozen cookies

Top to bottom: Coffee Chip Drops,
Chocolate Cheesecake Bars (page 84)

ULTIMATE CHOCOLATE CHIP COOKIES

Frosty's Colorful Cookies

1¼ cups firmly packed light
   brown sugar
¾ cup Butter Flavor Crisco
   all-vegetable shortening
   or ¾ Butter Flavor
   Crisco Stick
2 tablespoons milk

1 tablespoon vanilla
1 egg
1¾ cups all-purpose flour
1 teaspoon salt
¾ teaspoon baking soda
2 cups red and green candy-
   coated chocolate pieces

1. Heat oven to 375°F. Place sheets of foil on countertop for cooling cookies.

2. Place brown sugar, shortening, milk and vanilla in large bowl. Beat at medium speed of electric mixer until well blended. Add egg; beat well.

3. Combine flour, salt and baking soda. Add to shortening mixture; beat at low speed just until blended. Stir in candy-coated chocolate pieces.

4. Drop dough by rounded measuring tablespoonfuls 3 inches apart onto ungreased baking sheets.

5. Bake one baking sheet at a time at 375°F for 8 to 10 minutes for chewy cookies, or 11 to 13 minutes for crisp cookies. *Do not overbake.* Cool 2 minutes on baking sheet. Remove cookies to foil to cool completely.   *Makes about 3 dozen cookies*

Cherry Chocolate Chippies

1¼ cups firmly packed light
   brown sugar
¾ cup Butter Flavor Crisco
   all-vegetable shortening
   or ¾ Butter Flavor
   Crisco Stick
1 teaspoon vanilla
1 teaspoon almond extract
1 egg

1¾ cups all-purpose flour
1 teaspoon salt
¾ teaspoon baking soda
1 cup (6 ounces) semisweet
   chocolate chips
1 cup well-drained
   maraschino cherries,
   coarsely chopped

1. Heat oven to 375°F. Place sheets of foil on countertop for cooling cookies.

2. Place brown sugar, shortening, vanilla and almond extract in large bowl. Beat at medium speed of electric mixer until well blended. Add egg; beat well.

3. Combine flour, salt and baking soda. Add to shortening mixture; beat at low speed just until blended. Stir in chocolate chips and cherries.

4. Drop dough by rounded measuring tablespoonfuls 2 inches apart onto ungreased baking sheets.

5. Bake one baking sheet at a time at 375°F for 8 to 10 minutes for chewy cookies, or 11 to 13 minutes for crisp cookies. *Do not overbake.* Cool 2 minutes on baking sheet. Remove cookies to foil to cool completely. *Makes about 3 dozen cookies*

Peanut Butter Treats

1¼ cups firmly packed light
    brown sugar
¾ cup Butter Flavor Crisco
    all-vegetable shortening
    or ¾ Butter Flavor
    Crisco Stick
2 tablespoons milk
1 tablespoon vanilla
1 egg

1¾ cups all-purpose flour
1 teaspoon salt
¾ teaspoon baking soda
2 cups (about 32) miniature
    peanut butter cups,
    unwrapped and
    quartered or coarsely
    chopped

1. Heat oven to 375°F. Place sheets of foil on countertop for cooling cookies.

2. Place brown sugar, shortening, milk and vanilla in large bowl. Beat at medium speed of electric mixer until well blended. Add egg; beat well.

3. Combine flour, salt and baking soda. Add to shortening mixture; beat at low speed just until blended. Stir in peanut butter cup quarters.

4. Drop dough by rounded measuring tablespoonfuls 3 inches apart onto ungreased baking sheets.

5. Bake one baking sheet at a time at 375°F for 8 to 10 minutes or until cookies are lightly browned. *Do not overbake.* Cool 2 minutes on baking sheet. Remove cookies to foil to cool completely.
Makes about 3 dozen cookies

Orange-Glazed Date Nut Bars

Christmas is a great time for entertaining friends and family, but sometimes it's difficult to coordinate everyone's busy schedules. Why not plan an open house that will allow guests to stop in during their busy day? Set a buffet table with make-your-own sandwiches for early afternoon and prepare a large pot of spicy chili or hearty soup for evening. No matter what the menu, an assortment of make-ahead holiday cookies will be welcomed by all your guests.

Cookie Base

- 1¼ cups firmly packed light brown sugar
- ¾ cup Butter Flavor Crisco all-vegetable shortening or ¾ Butter Flavor Crisco Stick
- 2 tablespoons orange juice
- 1 tablespoon vanilla
- 1 tablespoon grated orange peel
- 1 egg
- 1¾ cups all-purpose flour
- 1 teaspoon salt
- ¾ teaspoon baking soda
- 1 cup chopped dates
- 1 cup chopped walnuts

Glaze

- 1½ cups confectioners sugar
- 2 tablespoons orange juice

1. Heat oven to 350°F. Grease 13 × 9-inch baking pan. Place cooling rack on counter.

2. Place brown sugar, shortening, orange juice, vanilla and orange peel in large bowl. Beat at medium speed of electric mixer until well blended. Add egg; beat well.

3. Combine flour, salt and baking soda. Add to shortening mixture; beat at low speed just until blended. Stir in dates and walnuts.

4. Press dough into prepared pan.

5. Bake at 350°F for 20 to 25 minutes or until lightly browned and firm. *Do not overbake.* Cool completely on cooling rack.

6. For glaze, combine confectioners sugar and orange juice. Stir until smooth. Spread glaze over cookie base. Cut into 2 × 1½-inch bars. Garnish if desired.

Makes 3 dozen bars

Top to bottom: Raspberry Linzer Rounds (page 57), Orange-Glazed Date Nut Bars

Pecan Praline Cookies

Praline
1½ cups chopped pecans
½ cup granulated sugar
3 tablespoons water

Cookies
1¼ cups firmly packed light
   brown sugar
¾ cup Butter Flavor Crisco
   all-vegetable shortening
   or ¾ Butter Flavor
   Crisco Stick

2 tablespoons milk
1 tablespoon vanilla
1 egg
1¾ cups all-purpose flour
1 teaspoon salt
¾ teaspoon baking soda

1. Heat oven to 375°F. Place sheets of foil on countertop for cooling cookies.

2. For praline, spread pecans on baking sheet; bake at 375°F for 10 minutes or until lightly toasted, stirring several times. Reserve pecans. Grease baking sheet.

3. Place granulated sugar and water in small saucepan. Bring to boil, stirring occasionally. Cover; boil 2 minutes. Uncover; cook 2 minutes or until mixture becomes golden brown in color. Add reserved pecans; stir until evenly coated. Spread on prepared baking sheet. Cool completely. Place hardened praline in heavy resealable plastic bag; seal. Crush with bottom of small heavy skillet until pieces are small.

4. For cookies, place brown sugar, shortening, milk and vanilla in large bowl. Beat at medium speed of electric mixer until well blended. Add egg; beat well.

5. Combine flour, salt and baking soda. Add to shortening mixture; beat at low speed just until blended. Stir in 1½ cups of crushed praline.

6. Shape dough into 1-inch balls. Dip top of each ball into remaining crushed praline. Place 3 inches apart on ungreased baking sheets.

7. Bake one baking sheet at a time at 375°F for 9 to 11 minutes or until cookies are lightly browned. *Do not overbake.* Cool 2 minutes on baking sheet. Remove cookies to foil to cool completely.

Makes about 3 dozen cookies

Pecan Praline Cookies

CHEWY OATMEAL COOKIES

Dotted with plump raisins and scented with cinnamon, classic oatmeal cookies have been around for most of the 20th century and had changed very little until the Crisco Kitchens developed the Chewy Oatmeal Cookie. What makes these so special is all there in the name—they are chewy and soft, so the nutty flavor and rich texture of the oatmeal does not leave a dry feel in the mouth.

The Crisco Kitchens have also found that Chewy Oatmeal Cookies are extremely versatile. Just by changing a few ingredients in this recipe, you can make a delightful array of new cookies all uniquely different from the basic recipe. Replace the raisins with pineapple and coconut and enjoy Aloha Oatmeal Cookies. Add grated carrots and chopped apple and discover Good 'n' Tasties. The variations are not limited to just drop cookies. This easy-to-make dough with a few simple changes can be pressed into a baking pan for the base of fabulous treats, such as Oatmeal Praline Cheese Bars and Peach Oatmeal Bars.

For those who think that a cookie isn't a cookie without a sweet-flavored chip, this chapter includes recipes with bits of chocolate and toffee. And like every other recipe in this chapter, they begin with the same easy basic recipe.

Chewy Oatmeal Cookies (page 28)

Chewy Oatmeal Cookies

1¼ cups firmly packed light
    brown sugar
¾ cup Butter Flavor Crisco
    all-vegetable shortening
    or ¾ Butter Flavor
    Crisco Stick
1 egg
⅓ cup milk
1½ teaspoons vanilla

3 cups quick oats, uncooked
1 cup all-purpose flour
½ teaspoon baking soda
½ teaspoon salt
¼ teaspoon cinnamon
1 cup raisins
1 cup coarsely chopped
    walnuts

1. Heat oven to 375°F. Grease baking sheets. Place sheets of foil on countertop for cooling cookies.

2. Place brown sugar, shortening, egg, milk and vanilla in large bowl. Beat at medium speed of electric mixer until well blended.

3. Combine oats, flour, baking soda, salt and cinnamon. Add to shortening mixture; beat at low speed just until blended. Stir in raisins and walnuts.

4. Drop dough by rounded measuring tablespoonfuls 2 inches apart onto prepared baking sheets.

5. Bake one baking sheet at a time at 375°F for 10 to 12 minutes or until cookies are lightly browned. *Do not overbake.* Cool 2 minutes on baking sheet. Remove cookies to foil to cool completely.

Makes about 2½ dozen cookies

Fall Harvest Oatmeal Cookies

1¼ cups firmly packed light brown sugar
¾ cup Butter Flavor Crisco all-vegetable shortening or ¾ Butter Flavor Crisco Stick
1 egg
⅓ cup milk
1 tablespoon grated orange peel
1½ teaspoons vanilla
3 cups quick oats, uncooked

1 cup all-purpose flour
1½ teaspoons cinnamon
½ teaspoon baking soda
½ teaspoon salt
¼ teaspoon nutmeg
¼ teaspoon ground cloves
1 cup coarsely chopped, peeled apples
1 cup raisins
1 cup coarsely chopped walnuts

1. Heat oven to 375°F. Grease baking sheets. Place sheets of foil on countertop for cooling cookies.

2. Place brown sugar, shortening, egg, milk, orange peel and vanilla in large bowl. Beat at medium speed of electric mixer until well blended.

3. Combine oats, flour, cinnamon, baking soda, salt, nutmeg and cloves. Add to shortening mixture; beat at low speed just until blended. Stir in apples, raisins and walnuts.

4. Drop dough by rounded measuring tablespoonfuls 2 inches apart onto prepared baking sheets.

5. Bake one baking sheet at a time at 375°F for 10 to 12 minutes or until cookies are lightly browned. *Do not overbake.* Cool 2 minutes on baking sheet. Remove cookies to foil to cool completely.

Makes about 2½ dozen cookies

Cranberry Nut Oatmeal Cookies

1¼ cups firmly packed light brown
    sugar
¾ cup Butter Flavor Crisco
    all-vegetable shortening
    or ¾ Butter Flavor Crisco Stick
1 egg
⅓ cup milk
1½ teaspoons vanilla
1 teaspoon grated orange peel
3 cups quick oats, uncooked
1 cup all-purpose flour
½ teaspoon baking soda
½ teaspoon salt
¼ teaspoon cinnamon
1 cup dried cranberries
1 cup coarsely chopped walnuts

1. Heat oven to 375°F. Grease baking
sheets. Place sheets of foil on countertop for
cooling cookies.

2. Place brown sugar, shortening, egg, milk,
vanilla and orange peel in large bowl. Beat at
medium speed of electric mixer until well
blended.

3. Combine oats, flour, baking soda, salt and
cinnamon. Add to shortening mixture; beat
at low speed just until blended. Stir in
cranberries and walnuts.

4. Drop dough by rounded measuring
tablespoonfuls 2 inches apart onto prepared
baking sheets.

5. Bake one baking sheet at a time at 375°F
for 10 to 12 minutes or until cookies are
lightly browned. *Do not overbake.* Cool
2 minutes on baking sheet. Remove cookies
to foil to cool completely.
Makes about 2½ dozen cookies

Top to Bottom: Fall Harvest
Oatmeal Cookies (page 29),
Cranberry Nut Oatmeal Cookies

*While cookies may
not be a tradition
at your
Thanksgiving
dinner, they should
have a place in the
day's festivities.
These cranberry
and nut-studded
cookies will quiet the
predinner hungries
or top off a late
evening snack. Fall
Harvest Oatmeal
Cookies will make a
great dessert for
even the most
finicky kid on your
guest list. No
matter which you
choose, these make-
ahead treats are
sure to please.*

Aloha Oatmeal Cookies

If friends are embarking on a special trip, send them off in style with a Bon Voyage Party. Serve cookies that are appropriate to their destination. These spicy cookies loaded with pineapple, coconut and macadamia nuts are great whether their destination is Hawaii or some other island paradise. Since cookies are such great travelers, wrap the extras for snacking on the trip.

1¼ cups firmly packed light brown sugar
¾ cup Butter Flavor Crisco all-vegetable shortening or ¾ Butter Flavor Crisco Stick
1 egg
2 tablespoons orange juice
1 tablespoon grated orange peel
1 teaspoon vanilla
½ teaspoon orange or lemon extract
3 cups quick oats, uncooked
1 cup all-purpose flour
½ teaspoon baking soda
½ teaspoon salt
½ teaspoon ground ginger
1 can (8 ounces) crushed pineapple in natural juice, well-drained
1 cup flaked coconut
1 cup chopped macadamia nuts

1. Heat oven to 375°F. Grease baking sheets. Place sheets of foil on countertop for cooling cookies.

2. Place brown sugar, shortening, egg, orange juice, orange peel, vanilla and orange extract in large bowl. Beat at medium speed of electric mixer until well blended.

3. Combine oats, flour, baking soda, salt and ginger. Add to shortening mixture; beat at low speed just until blended. Stir in pineapple, coconut and macadamia nuts.

4. Drop dough by rounded measuring tablespoonfuls 2 inches apart onto prepared baking sheets.

5. Bake one baking sheet at a time at 375°F for 10 to 12 minutes or until cookies are lightly browned. *Do not overbake.* Cool 2 minutes. Remove cookies to foil to cool.
Makes about 2½ dozen cookies

Aloha Oatmeal Cookies

CHEWY OATMEAL COOKIES

Oatmeal Praline Cheese Bars

Cookie Base

1¼ cups firmly packed light
    brown sugar
¾ cup Butter Flavor Crisco
    all-vegetable shortening
    or ¾ Butter Flavor
    Crisco Stick
1 egg
⅓ cup milk
1½ teaspoons vanilla
1½ cups quick oats, uncooked
1 cup all-purpose flour
1 cup finely chopped pecans
¼ cup toasted wheat germ
½ teaspoon baking soda
½ teaspoon salt
½ teaspoon cinnamon

Topping

1 package (8 ounces) cream
    cheese, softened
⅓ cup firmly packed light
    brown sugar
2 eggs
2 tablespoons all-purpose
    flour
½ teaspoon vanilla
¼ teaspoon salt
½ cup almond brickle chips
½ cup finely chopped pecans

1. Heat oven to 350°F. Grease 13 × 9-inch baking pan. Place cooling rack on countertop.

2. For cookie base, place brown sugar, shortening, egg, milk and vanilla in large bowl. Beat at medium speed of electric mixer until well blended.

3. Combine oats, flour, pecans, wheat germ, baking soda, salt and cinnamon. Add to shortening mixture; beat at low speed just until blended.

4. Spread dough onto bottom of prepared pan.

5. Bake at 350°F for 15 to 17 minutes or until surface is light golden brown and edges pull away from sides of pan. *Do not overbake.*

6. For topping, place cream cheese, brown sugar, eggs, flour, vanilla and salt in medium bowl. Beat at medium speed of electric mixer until smooth. Pour mixture over cookie base. Sprinkle with almond brickle chips and pecans.

7. Bake 15 to 17 minutes longer or until topping is set. *Do not overbake.* Cool completely on cooling rack. Cut into 2 × 1½-inch bars. Refrigerate.

Makes about 3 dozen bars

Top to bottom: Cappuccino Cookies
(page 54), Oatmeal Praline
Cheese Bars

Chocolate Cherry Oatmeal Fancies

Everyone loves cookie baking and spending time with loved ones around the holidays. Why not combine the two and invite a group for a cookie-baking session? Ask your guests to bring their favorite recipes. Spend the day baking and everyone goes home with a fantastic assortment of cookies.

½ cup sliced almonds
1¼ cups firmly packed light brown sugar
¾ cup Butter Flavor Crisco all-vegetable shortening or ¾ Butter Flavor Crisco Stick
1 egg
⅓ cup milk
1 teaspoon vanilla
½ teaspoon almond extract
3 cups quick oats, uncooked
1 cup all-purpose flour
½ teaspoon baking soda
½ teaspoon salt
6 ounces white baking chocolate, coarsely chopped
6 ounces semisweet chocolate, coarsely chopped
½ cup coarsely chopped red candied cherries or well-drained, chopped maraschino cherries

1. Heat oven to 350°F. Spread almonds on baking sheet. Bake at 350°F for 5 to 7 minutes or until almonds are golden brown. Cool completely; reserve.

2. *Increase oven temperature to 375°F.* Grease baking sheets. Place sheets of foil on countertop for cooling cookies.

3. Place brown sugar, shortening, egg, milk, vanilla and almond extract in large bowl. Beat at medium speed of electric mixer until well blended.

4. Combine oats, flour, baking soda and salt. Add to shortening mixture; beat at low speed just until blended. Stir in white chocolate, semisweet chocolate, cherries and reserved almonds.

5. Drop dough by rounded measuring tablespoonfuls 2 inches apart onto prepared baking sheets.

6. Bake one baking sheet at a time at 375°F for 10 to 12 minutes or until cookies are lightly browned. *Do not overbake.* Cool 2 minutes on baking sheet. Remove cookies to foil to cool completely.

Makes about 4 dozen cookies

Good 'n' Tasties

1¼ cups firmly packed light brown sugar
¾ cup Butter Flavor Crisco all-vegetable shortening or ¾ Butter Flavor Crisco Stick
1 egg
⅓ cup milk
1 tablespoon grated orange peel
1½ teaspoons vanilla
1½ cups quick oats, uncooked
1 cup whole-wheat flour
½ cup all-purpose flour
¼ cup toasted wheat germ
1½ teaspoons cinnamon
1 teaspoon baking soda
½ teaspoon salt
1 cup raisins
1 cup coarsely chopped walnuts or pecans
1 apple, peeled and coarsely chopped
½ cup grated carrots
½ cup flaked coconut

1. Heat oven to 375°F. Grease baking sheets. Place sheets of foil on countertop for cooling cookies.

2. Place brown sugar, shortening, egg, milk, orange peel and vanilla in large bowl. Beat at medium speed of electric mixer until well blended.

3. Combine oats, whole-wheat flour, all-purpose flour, wheat germ, cinnamon, baking soda and salt. Add to shortening mixture; beat at low speed just until blended. Stir in raisins, walnuts, apple, carrots and coconut.

4. Drop dough by rounded measuring tablespoonfuls 2 inches apart onto prepared baking sheets.

5. Bake one baking sheet at a time at 375°F for 10 to 12 minutes or until cookies are lightly browned. *Do not overbake.* Cool 2 minutes on baking sheet. Remove cookies to foil to cool completely.

Makes about 3½ dozen cookies

Peach Oatmeal Bars

Summer is naturally a time for friends and family to gather. Plan a picnic or barbecue for Memorial Day, Fourth of July or Labor Day. Just be sure the menu includes an assortment of easy-to-transport cookies—chewy Peach Oatmeal Bars, refreshing Tropical Lime Cookies or Cracked Chocolate Cookies loaded with bits of chocolate.

1¼ cups firmly packed light brown sugar
¾ cup Butter Flavor Crisco all-vegetable shortening or ¾ Butter Flavor Crisco Stick
1 egg
2 tablespoons milk
1 teaspoon vanilla
½ teaspoon almond extract
3 cups quick oats, uncooked
1 cup all-purpose flour
½ teaspoon baking soda
½ teaspoon salt
½ teaspoon ground ginger
1 can (16 ounces) sliced peaches, drained and finely chopped
1 cup peach preserves or jam, stirred

1. Heat oven to 350°F. Grease 15½ × 10½ × 1-inch jelly-roll pan.

2. Place brown sugar, shortening, egg, milk, vanilla and almond extract in large bowl. Beat at medium speed of electric mixer until well blended.

3. Combine oats, flour, baking soda, salt and ginger. Add to shortening mixture; beat at low speed just until blended. Stir in chopped peaches.

4. Spread ½ of dough onto bottom of prepared pan. Spread preserves over dough. Drop remaining dough by spoonfuls over preserves. Spread dough.

5. Bake at 350°F for 30 to 35 minutes or until golden brown. *Do not overbake.* Loosen from sides of pan with knife. Cool completely on cooling rack. Cut into 2 × 1½-inch bars.   *Makes about 4 dozen bars*

Clockwise from top left: Peach Oatmeal Bars, Cracked Chocolate Cookies (page 90), Tropical Lime Cookies (page 55)

Chewy Oatmeal Trail Mix Cookies

1¼ cups firmly packed light brown
  sugar
¾ cup Butter Flavor Crisco all-
  vegetable shortening or ¾ Butter
  Flavor Crisco Stick
1 egg
⅓ cup milk
1½ teaspoons vanilla
2½ cups quick oats, uncooked
1 cup all-purpose flour
½ teaspoon baking soda
½ teaspoon salt
¼ teaspoon cinnamon
1 cup (6 ounces) semisweet or milk
  chocolate chips
¾ cup raisins
¾ cup coarsely chopped nuts
½ cup sunflower seeds

1. Heat oven to 375°F. Grease baking sheets. Place sheets of foil on countertop.

2. Place brown sugar, shortening, egg, milk and vanilla in large bowl. Beat at medium speed of electric mixer until well blended.

3. Combine oats, flour, baking soda, salt and cinnamon. Add to shortening mixture; beat at low speed just until blended. Stir in chocolate chips, raisins, nuts and sunflower seeds.

4. Drop dough by rounded measuring tablespoonfuls 2 inches apart onto prepared baking sheets.

5. Bake one baking sheet at a time at 375°F for 10 to 12 minutes or until cookies are lightly browned. *Do not overbake.* Cool 2 minutes. Remove cookies to foil to cool completely.   *Makes about 3 dozen cookies*

These cookies will practically beg to be taken along on your next camping or hiking expedition or trip to the beach. They are chock-full of goodies that will satisfy your hunger.

3 cups of prepared trail mix (available in grocery or health food stores) can be substituted for the chocolate chips, raisins, nuts and sunflower seeds.

Chewy Oatmeal Trail Mix Cookies

ULTIMATE SUGAR COOKIES

In the past, sugar cookies were primarily seen as blank canvases begging to be decorated for the holidays. Although pretty, few of us liked the flavor or texture of the cookie. Now meet the Ultimate Sugar Cookie! It was developed by the Crisco Kitchens to be so moist, and above all so delectable, that it will become one of your favorites. And now it is less likely to crumble when iced than a crisper cookie made with butter or margarine. This makes it the ideal cookie for cutting into shapes and decorating.

Browse through this chapter and discover how versatile this recipe can be. With minor variations, you can have a great array of scrumptious cookies in a seemingly endless variety of shapes. You and your family can travel the world right in your kitchen— from the intriguing Scandinavian flavor of Orange-Cardamom Thins to Southwestern Bizcochitos, fragrant with anise. And don't miss the delightful Jammy Pinwheels and fantastic Frosted Easter Cut-outs.

So forget your old notions about sugar cookies and discover the whole new world of Ultimate Sugar Cookies—dazzling to the taste buds and exquisite to behold.

Ultimate Sugar Cookies (page 44)

Ultimate Sugar Cookies

1¼ cups granulated sugar
  1 cup Butter Flavor Crisco
    all-vegetable shortening
    or 1 Butter Flavor
    Crisco Stick
  2 eggs
  ¼ cup light corn syrup or
    regular pancake syrup
  1 tablespoon vanilla

3 cups all-purpose flour
    (plus 4 tablespoons),
    divided
¾ teaspoon baking powder
½ teaspoon baking soda
½ teaspoon salt
  Granulated sugar or
    colored sugar crystals

1. Place sugar and shortening in large bowl. Beat at medium speed of electric mixer until well blended. Add eggs, syrup and vanilla; beat until well blended and fluffy.

2. Combine 3 cups flour, baking powder, baking soda and salt. Add gradually to shortening mixture, beating at low speed until well blended.

3. Divide dough into 4 equal pieces; shape each piece into disk. Wrap with plastic wrap. Refrigerate 1 hour or until firm.

4. Heat oven to 375°F. Place sheets of foil on countertop for cooling cookies.

5. Sprinkle about 1 tablespoon flour on large sheet of waxed paper. Place disk of dough on floured paper; flatten slightly with hands. Turn dough over; cover with another large sheet of waxed paper. Roll dough to ¼-inch thickness. Remove top sheet of waxed paper. Cut into desired shapes with floured cookie cutters. Place 2 inches apart on ungreased baking sheet. Repeat with remaining dough.

6. Sprinkle with granulated sugar.

7. Bake one baking sheet at a time at 375°F for 5 to 7 minutes or until edges of cookies are lightly browned. *Do not overbake.* Cool 2 minutes on baking sheet. Remove cookies to foil to cool completely.

Makes about 3½ dozen cookies

Orange-Cardamom Thins

1¼ cups granulated sugar
1 cup Butter Flavor Crisco
    all-vegetable shortening
    or 1 Butter Flavor Crisco Stick
1 egg
¼ cup light corn syrup or regular
    pancake syrup
1 teaspoon vanilla
1 tablespoon grated orange peel
½ teaspoon orange extract
3 cups all-purpose flour
1¼ teaspoons cardamom
¾ teaspoon baking powder
½ teaspoon baking soda
½ teaspoon salt
½ teaspoon cinnamon

Cardamom, a member of the ginger family, has a pungent aroma and a spicy-sweet flavor. It is used most often in Scandinavian and East Indian cooking.

1. Place sugar and shortening in large bowl. Beat at medium speed of electric mixer until well blended. Add egg, syrup, vanilla, orange peel and orange extract; beat until well blended and fluffy.

2. Combine flour, cardamom, baking powder, baking soda, salt and cinnamon. Add gradually to shortening mixture, beating at low speed until well blended.

3. Divide dough in half. Roll each half into 12-inch-long log. Wrap with plastic wrap. Refrigerate for 4 hours or until firm.

4. Heat oven to 375°F. Grease baking sheets. Place sheets of foil on counter for cooling cookies.

5. Cut rolls into ¼-inch-thick slices. Place 1 inch apart on prepared baking sheets.

6. Bake one baking sheet at a time at 375°F for 7 to 9 minutes or until bottoms of cookies are lightly browned. *Do not overbake.* Cool 2 minutes on baking sheet. Remove cookies to foil to cool completely.
        Makes about 5 dozen cookies

Toffee Spattered Sugar Stars

1¼ cups granulated sugar
1 cup Butter Flavor Crisco all-vegetable shortening or 1 Butter Flavor Crisco Stick
2 eggs
¼ cup light corn syrup or regular pancake syrup
1 tablespoon vanilla

3 cups all-purpose flour (plus 4 tablespoons), divided
¾ teaspoon baking powder
½ teaspoon baking soda
½ teaspoon salt
1 package (6 ounces) milk chocolate English toffee chips, divided

1. Place sugar and shortening in large bowl. Beat at medium speed of electric mixer until well blended. Add eggs, syrup and vanilla; beat until well blended and fluffy.

2. Combine 3 cups flour, baking powder, baking soda and salt. Add gradually to shortening mixture, beating at low speed until well blended.

3. Divide dough into 4 equal pieces; shape each into disk. Wrap with plastic wrap. Refrigerate 1 hour or until firm.

4. Heat oven to 375°F. Place sheets of foil on countertop for cooling cookies.

5. Sprinkle about 1 tablespoon flour on large sheet of waxed paper. Place disk of dough on floured paper; flatten slightly with hands. Turn dough over; cover with another large sheet of waxed paper. Roll dough to ¼-inch thickness. Remove top sheet of waxed paper. Sprinkle about ¼ of toffee chips over dough. Roll lightly into dough. Cut out with floured star or round cookie cutter. Place 2 inches apart on ungreased baking sheet. Repeat with remaining dough and toffee chips.

6. Bake one baking sheet at a time at 375°F for 5 to 7 minutes or until cookies are lightly browned around edges. *Do not overbake.* Cool 2 minutes on baking sheet. Remove cookies to foil to cool completely.

Makes about 3½ dozen cookies

Top to bottom: Pecan Cookies (page 54), Toffee Spattered Sugar Stars

Jammy Pinwheels

1¼ cups granulated sugar
1 cup Butter Flavor Crisco
   all-vegetable shortening
   or 1 Butter Flavor
   Crisco Stick
2 eggs
¼ cup light corn syrup or
   regular pancake syrup
1 tablespoon vanilla

3 cups all-purpose flour
   (plus 2 tablespoons),
   divided
¾ teaspoon baking powder
½ teaspoon baking soda
½ teaspoon salt
1 cup apricot, strawberry or
   seedless raspberry jam

1. Place sugar and shortening in large bowl. Beat at medium speed of electric mixer until well blended. Add eggs, syrup and vanilla; beat until well blended and fluffy.

2. Combine 3 cups flour, baking powder, baking soda and salt. Add gradually to shortening mixture, beating at low speed until well blended.

3. Divide dough in half. Pat each half into thick rectangle. Sprinkle about 1 tablespoon flour on large sheet of waxed paper. Place rectangle of dough on floured paper. Turn dough over; cover with another large sheet of waxed paper. Roll dough into an 8 × 12-inch rectangle about ⅛ inch thick. Trim edges. Slide dough and waxed paper onto ungreased baking sheets. Refrigerate 20 minutes or until firm. Repeat with remaining dough.

4. Heat oven to 375°F. Grease baking sheets. Place sheets of foil on counter for cooling cookies.

5. Place chilled dough rectangle on work surface. Remove top sheet of waxed paper. Cut dough into 2-inch squares. Place squares 2 inches apart on prepared baking sheets. Make a 1-inch diagonal cut from each corner of square almost to center. Place 1 teaspoon jam in center. Lift every other corner and bring together in center of cookie. Repeat with remaining dough.

6. Bake at 375°F for 7 to 10 minutes or until edges of cookies are golden brown. *Do not overbake.* Cool 2 minutes on baking sheet. Remove cookies to foil to cool completely.

Makes about 4 dozen cookies

*Clockwise from top left: Jammy
Pinwheels, Chocolate Cherry
Oatmeal Fancies (page 36),
Southwestern Bizcochitos (page 50)*

Southwestern Bizcochitos

Cookies

1¼ cups granulated sugar
1 cup Butter Flavor Crisco all-vegetable shortening or 1 Butter Flavor Crisco Stick
2 eggs
¼ cup light corn syrup or regular pancake syrup
1 tablespoon vanilla
1 tablespoon grated orange peel
2 teaspoons anise seed

3 cups all-purpose flour (plus 4 tablespoons), divided
¾ teaspoon baking powder
½ teaspoon baking soda
½ teaspoon salt

Topping

⅓ cup granulated sugar
1 tablespoon cinnamon
Milk

1. For cookies, place sugar and shortening in large bowl. Beat at medium speed of electric mixer until well blended. Add eggs, syrup, vanilla, orange peel and anise seed; beat until well blended and fluffy.

2. Combine 3 cups flour, baking powder, baking soda and salt. Add gradually to shortening mixture, beating at low speed until well blended. Wrap dough in plastic wrap. Refrigerate 1 hour or overnight.

3. Divide dough into 4 equal pieces; shape each into a disk. Wrap with plastic wrap. Refrigerate 1 hour or until firm.

4. Heat oven to 375°F. Place sheets of foil on countertop for cooling cookies.

5. Sprinkle about 1 tablespoon of flour on large sheet of waxed paper. Place disk of dough on floured paper; flatten slightly with hands. Turn dough over; cover with another large sheet of waxed paper. Roll dough to ¼-inch thickness. Remove top sheet of waxed paper. Cut out with floured cookie cutter. Place 2 inches apart on ungreased baking sheet. Repeat with remaining dough.

6. For topping, combine sugar and cinnamon. Brush cookies with milk. Sprinkle cookies with sugar mixture.

7. Bake one baking sheet at a time at 375°F for 7 to 9 minutes or until cookies are lightly set. *Do not overbake*. Cool 2 minutes on baking sheet. Remove cookies to foil to cool completely.

Makes about 4½ dozen cookies

Spritz Cookies

1¼ cups granulated sugar
1 cup Butter Flavor Crisco
    all-vegetable shortening
    or 1 Butter Flavor
    Crisco Stick
2 eggs
¼ cup light corn syrup or
    regular pancake syrup
1 tablespoon vanilla

3 cups all-purpose flour
¾ teaspoon baking powder
½ teaspoon baking soda
½ teaspoon salt
Colored sugar crystals
    (optional)
Nonpareils (optional)
Chocolate jimmies
    (optional)

1. Heat oven to 375°F. Place sheets of foil on countertop for cooling cookies.

2. Place sugar and shortening in large bowl. Beat at medium speed of electric mixer until well blended. Add eggs, syrup and vanilla; beat until well blended and fluffy.

3. Combine flour, baking powder, baking soda and salt. Add gradually to shortening mixture; beat at low speed until well blended.

4. Fill cookie press with dough, following manufacturer's directions. Press dough about 1½ inches apart on ungreased baking sheet. Sprinkle with colored sugar, nonpareils or chocolate jimmies, if desired.

5. Bake one sheet at a time at 375°F for 7 to 9 minutes or until bottoms of cookies are golden. *Do not overbake.* Cool 2 minutes on baking sheet. Remove cookies to foil to cool completely.

Makes about 7½ dozen cookies

Frosted Easter Cut-outs

Cookies
1¼ cups granulated sugar
1 cup Butter Flavor Crisco
all-vegetable shortening
or 1 Butter Flavor
Crisco Stick
2 eggs
¼ cup light corn syrup or
regular pancake syrup
1 tablespoon vanilla
3 cups all-purpose flour
(plus 4 tablespoons),
divided

¾ teaspoon baking powder
½ teaspoon baking soda
½ teaspoon salt

Icing
1 cup confectioners sugar
2 tablespoons milk
Food color (optional)
Decorating icing

1. Place sugar and shortening in large bowl. Beat at medium speed of electric mixer until well blended. Add eggs, syrup and vanilla; beat until well blended and fluffy.

2. Combine 3 cups flour, baking powder, baking soda and salt. Add gradually to shortening mixture, beating at low speed until well blended.

3. Divide dough into 4 equal pieces; shape each into disk. Wrap with plastic wrap. Refrigerate 1 hour or until firm.

4. Heat oven to 375°F. Place sheets of foil on countertop for cooling cookies.

5. Sprinkle about 1 tablespoon flour on large sheet of waxed paper. Place disk of dough on floured paper; flatten slightly with hands. Turn dough over; cover with another large sheet of waxed paper. Roll dough to ¼-inch thickness. Remove top sheet of waxed paper. Cut into desired shapes with floured cookie cutter. Place 2 inches apart on ungreased baking sheet. Repeat with remaining dough.

6. Bake one baking sheet at a time at 375°F for 5 to 7 minutes or until edges of cookies are lightly browned. *Do not overbake.* Cool 2 minutes on baking sheet. Remove cookies to foil to cool completely.

7. For icing, combine confectioners sugar and milk; stir until smooth. Add food color, if desired. Stir until blended. Spread icing on cookies; place on foil until icing is set. Decorate as desired with decorating icing.
Makes about 3½ dozen cookies

Frosted Easter Cut-outs

Pecan Cookies

1¼ cups confectioners sugar
1 cup Butter Flavor Crisco
   all-vegetable shortening
   or 1 Butter Flavor
   Crisco Stick
2 eggs
¼ cup light corn syrup or
   regular pancake syrup

1 tablespoon vanilla
2 cups all-purpose flour
1½ cups finely chopped
   pecans
¾ teaspoon baking powder
½ teaspoon baking soda
½ teaspoon salt
Confectioners sugar

1. Heat oven to 350°F. Place sheets of foil on countertop for cooling cookies.

2. Place confectioners sugar and shortening in large bowl. Beat at medium speed of electric mixer until well blended. Add eggs, syrup and vanilla; beat until well blended and fluffy.

3. Combine flour, pecans, baking powder, baking soda and salt. Add to shortening mixture; beat at low speed until well blended.

4. Shape dough into 1-inch balls. Place 2 inches apart on ungreased baking sheet.

5. Bake at 350°F for 15 to 18 minutes or until bottoms of cookies are light golden brown. *Do not overbake.* Cool 2 minutes on baking sheet. Roll in confectioners sugar while warm. Remove cookies to foil to cool completely. Reroll in confectioners sugar prior to serving.

Makes about 4 dozen cookies

Cappuccino Cookies

1¼ cups firmly packed light
   brown sugar
1 cup Butter Flavor Crisco
   all-vegetable shortening
   or 1 Butter Flavor
   Crisco Stick
2 eggs
¼ cup light corn syrup or
   regular pancake syrup
1 teaspoon vanilla

1 teaspoon rum extract
2 tablespoons instant
   espresso or coffee
   powder
3 cups all-purpose flour
¾ teaspoon baking powder
½ teaspoon baking soda
½ teaspoon salt
½ teaspoon nutmeg
Chocolate jimmies

1. Place brown sugar and shortening in large bowl. Beat at medium speed of electric mixer until well blended. Add eggs, corn syrup, vanilla, rum extract and coffee; beat until well blended and fluffy.

2. Combine flour, baking powder, baking soda, salt and nutmeg. Add gradually to shortening mixture, beating at low speed until blended. Divide dough in half. Roll each half into two logs approximately 2 inches in diameter. Wrap in waxed paper. Refrigerate several hours.

3. Heat oven to 350°F. Place sheets of foil on countertop for cooling cookies.

4. Cut cookies into ¼-inch-thick slices. Place 2 inches apart on ungreased baking sheet. Sprinkle center of each cookie with jimmies.

5. Bake one baking sheet at a time at 350°F for 10 to 12 minutes or until golden brown. *Do not overbake*. Cool 2 minutes. Remove cookies to foil to cool completely.   *Makes about 4½ dozen cookies*

Tropical Lime Cookies

1¼ cups confectioners sugar
1 cup Butter Flavor Crisco
   all-vegetable shortening
   or 1 Butter Flavor
   Crisco Stick
1 egg
¼ cup light corn syrup or
   regular pancake syrup
2 tablespoons lime juice

2 tablespoons grated lime
   peel (about 2 limes)
2½ cups all-purpose flour
¾ teaspoon baking powder
½ teaspoon baking soda
½ teaspoon salt
1 cup flaked coconut
Confectioners sugar

1. Heat oven to 325°F. Place sheets of foil on countertop for cooling cookies.

2. Place confectioners sugar and shortening in large bowl. Beat at medium speed of electric mixer until well blended. Add egg, syrup, lime juice and lime peel; beat until well blended and fluffy.

3. Combine flour, baking powder, baking soda and salt. Add gradually to shortening mixture, beating at low speed until well blended. Stir in coconut.

4. Shape dough into 1-inch balls. Place 2 inches apart on ungreased baking sheet.

5. Bake one baking sheet at a time at 325°F for 15 to 18 minutes or until bottoms of cookies are light golden brown. *Do not overbake*. Cool 2 minutes on baking sheet. Remove cookies to foil. Dust warm cookies with confectioners sugar. Cool completely. Garnish as desired.

Makes about 5 dozen cookies

Maple Pecan Sandwich Cookies

Cookies

1¼ cups firmly packed light
  brown sugar
1 cup Butter Flavor Crisco
  all-vegetable shortening
  or 1 Butter Flavor
  Crisco Stick
2 eggs
¼ cup maple syrup or maple
  flavored pancake syrup
1 teaspoon maple extract
½ teaspoon vanilla
2½ cups all-purpose flour
  (plus 4 tablespoons),
  divided
1½ cups finely ground pecans

¾ teaspoon baking powder
½ teaspoon baking soda
½ teaspoon salt
20 to 30 pecan halves
  (optional)

Filling

1¼ cups confectioners sugar
3 tablespoons Butter Flavor
  Crisco all-vegetable
  shortening
1 teaspoon maple extract
  Dash salt
2½ teaspoons milk

1. For cookies, place brown sugar and shortening in large bowl. Beat at medium speed of electric mixer until well blended. Add eggs, syrup, maple extract and vanilla; beat until well blended and fluffy.

2. Combine 2½ cups flour, ground pecans, baking powder, baking soda and salt. Add gradually to shortening mixture, beating at low speed until well blended.

3. Divide dough into 4 equal pieces; shape each into disk. Wrap with plastic wrap. Refrigerate 1 hour or until firm.

4. Heat oven to 375°F. Place sheets of foil on countertop for cooling cookies.

5. Sprinkle about 1 tablespoon flour on large sheet of waxed paper. Place disk of dough on floured paper; flatten slightly with hands. Turn dough over; cover with another large sheet of waxed paper. Roll dough to ¼-inch thickness. Cut out with floured 3-inch scalloped round cookie cutter. Place 2 inches apart on ungreased baking sheet. Roll out remaining dough. Place pecans in center of half of cookies, if desired.

6. Bake one baking sheet at a time at 375°F for 5 to 7 minutes or until lightly browned around edges. *Do not overbake.* Cool 2 minutes on baking sheet. Remove cookies to foil to cool completely.

7. For filling, place confectioners sugar, shortening, maple extract and salt in medium bowl. Beat at low speed until smooth. Add milk; beat until mixture is smooth. Spread filling on flat side of 1 plain cookie. Cover with flat side of second cookie with pecan. Repeat with remaining cookies and filling. Garnish as desired.

Makes about 2 dozen sandwich cookies

Raspberry Linzer Rounds

1¼ cups granulated sugar
1 cup Butter Flavor Crisco
    all-vegetable shortening
    or 1 Butter Flavor
    Crisco Stick
2 eggs
¼ cup light corn syrup or
    regular pancake syrup
1 teaspoon vanilla
1 teaspoon almond extract
3 cups all-purpose flour
    (plus 4 tablespoons),
    divided

1 cup ground almonds
    (about 4 to 5 ounces)
¾ teaspoon baking powder
½ teaspoon baking soda
½ teaspoon salt
½ cup seedless raspberry
    preserves, stirred
Confectioners sugar
    (optional)

1. Place granulated sugar and shortening in large bowl. Beat at medium speed of electric mixer until well blended. Add eggs, syrup, vanilla and almond extract; beat until well blended and fluffy.

2. Combine 3 cups flour, ground almonds, baking powder, baking soda and salt. Add gradually to shortening mixture, beating at low speed until well blended.

3. Divide dough into 4 pieces; shape each piece into disk. Wrap with plastic wrap. Refrigerate several hours or until firm.

4. Heat oven to 375°F. Place sheets of foil on countertop for cooling cookies.

5. Sprinkle about 1 tablespoon flour on large sheet of waxed paper. Place disk of dough on floured paper; flatten slightly with hands. Turn dough over and cover with another large sheet of waxed paper. Roll dough to ¼-inch thickness. Remove top sheet of waxed paper. Cut out with 2- or 2½-inch floured scalloped round cookie cutter. Place 2 inches apart on ungreased baking sheet. Repeat with remaining dough. Cut out centers of half the cookies with ½- or ¾-inch round cutter.

6. Bake one baking sheet at a time at 375°F for 5 to 7 minutes or until edges of cookies are lightly browned.* *Do not overbake.* Cool 2 minutes on baking sheet. Remove cookies to foil to cool completely.

7. Spread a small amount of raspberry jam on bottom of solid cookies; cover with cut-out cookies, bottom sides down, to form sandwiches. Sift confectioners sugar, if desired, over tops of cookies.

Makes about 2 dozen cookies

*Bake larger cookies 1 to 2 minutes longer.

St. Pat's Pinwheels

1¼ cups granulated sugar
1 cup Butter Flavor Crisco
   all-vegetable shortening
   or 1 Butter Flavor
   Crisco Stick
2 eggs
¼ cup light corn syrup or
   regular pancake syrup
1 tablespoon vanilla

3 cups all-purpose flour
   (plus 2 tablespoons),
   divided
¾ teaspoon baking powder
½ teaspoon baking soda
½ teaspoon salt
½ teaspoon peppermint
   extract
Green food color

1. Place sugar and shortening in large bowl. Beat at medium speed of electric mixer until well blended. Add eggs, syrup and vanilla; beat until well blended and fluffy.

2. Combine 3 cups flour, baking powder, baking soda and salt. Add gradually to shortening mixture, beating at low speed until well blended.

3. Place half of dough in medium bowl. Stir in peppermint extract and food color, a few drops at a time, until of desired shade of green. Shape each dough into disk. Wrap with plastic wrap. Refrigerate several hours or until firm.

4. Sprinkle about 1 tablespoon flour on large sheet of waxed paper. Place peppermint dough on floured paper; flatten slightly with hands. Turn dough over; cover with another large sheet of waxed paper. Roll dough into 14 × 9-inch rectangle. Set aside. Repeat with plain dough.

5. Remove top sheet of waxed paper from both doughs. Invert plain dough onto peppermint dough, aligning edges carefully. Roll layers together lightly. Remove waxed paper from plain dough. Trim dough to form rectangle. Roll dough tightly in jelly-roll fashion starting with long side and using bottom sheet of waxed paper as guide, removing waxed paper during rolling. Wrap roll in waxed paper; freeze at least 30 minutes or until very firm.

6. Heat oven to 375°F. Place sheets of foil on countertop for cooling cookies.

7. Remove roll from freezer; remove wrapping. Cut roll into ⅜-inch-thick slices. Place slices 2 inches apart on ungreased baking sheet.

8. Bake one baking sheet at a time at 375°F for 7 to 9 minutes or until edges of cookies are very lightly browned. *Do not overbake.* Cool 2 minutes on baking sheet. Remove cookies to foil to cool completely.
Makes about 3 dozen cookies

St. Pat's Pinwheels

Lollipop Cookies

Cookies

1¼ cups granulated sugar
1 cup Butter Flavor Crisco all-vegetable shortening or 1 Butter Flavor Crisco Stick
2 eggs
¼ cup light corn syrup or regular pancake syrup
1 tablespoon vanilla
3 cups all-purpose flour
¾ teaspoon baking powder
½ teaspoon baking soda
½ teaspoon salt
36 flat ice cream sticks

Decorations

Any of the following: miniature baking chips, raisins, red hots, nonpareils, colored sugar or nuts

1. Place sugar and shortening in large bowl. Beat at medium speed of electric mixer until well blended. Add eggs, syrup and vanilla; beat until well blended and fluffy.

2. Combine flour, baking powder, baking soda and salt. Add gradually to shortening mixture, beating at low speed until well blended. Cover; refrigerate for several hours or until firm.

3. Heat oven to 375°F. Place sheets of foil on countertop for cooling cookies.

4. Shape dough into 1½-inch balls. Push ice cream stick into center of dough. Place dough 3 inches apart on ungreased baking sheet with stick parallel to baking sheet. Flatten dough to ½-inch thickness with bottom of greased and floured glass. Decorate as desired; press decorations gently into dough.

5. Bake at 375°F for 8 to 10 minutes. *Do not overbake.* Cool on baking sheet 2 minutes. Remove cookies to foil to cool completely.

Makes about 3 dozen cookies

Lemon-Poppy Seed Cookies

1¼ cups granulated sugar
1 cup Butter Flavor Crisco all-vegetable shortening or 1 Butter Flavor Crisco Stick
2 eggs
¼ cup light corn syrup or regular pancake syrup
2 tablespoons poppy seeds
1 tablespoon grated lemon peel

1½ teaspoons pure lemon extract
1 teaspoon vanilla
3 cups all-purpose flour (plus 4 tablespoons), divided
1 teaspoon ground ginger
¾ teaspoon baking powder
½ teaspoon baking soda
½ teaspoon salt

1. Place sugar and shortening in large bowl. Beat at medium speed of electric mixer until well blended. Add eggs, syrup, poppy seeds, lemon peel, lemon extract and vanilla; beat until well blended and fluffy.

2. Combine 3 cups flour, ginger, baking powder, baking soda and salt. Add gradually to shortening mixture, beating at low speed until well blended.

3. Divide dough into 4 equal pieces; shape each piece into disk. Wrap with plastic wrap. Refrigerate 1 hour or until firm.

4. Heat oven to 375°F. Place sheets of foil on countertop for cooling cookies.

5. Sprinkle about 1 tablespoon flour on large sheet of waxed paper. Place disk of dough on floured paper; flatten slightly with hands. Turn dough over; cover with another large sheet of waxed paper. Roll dough to ⅛-inch thickness. Remove top sheet of waxed paper. Cut out with floured scalloped round or heart cookie cutters. Place 2 inches apart on ungreased baking sheet. Repeat with remaining dough.

6. Bake one baking sheet at a time at 375°F for 5 to 6 minutes or until edges of cookies just begin to brown. *Do not overbake.* Cool 2 minutes on baking sheet. Remove cookies to foil to cool completely.

Makes about 6½ dozen cookies

IRRESISTIBLE PEANUT BUTTER COOKIES

Peanut butter cookies are instantly recognized by their familiar crosshatch pattern. But beneath those lines, Crisco's Irresistible Peanut Butter Cookies are brimming with peanut butter flavor. They deliver the maximum in peanut taste as well as the soft moist texture that you prefer.

While the basic Irresistible Peanut Butter Cookie is a favorite with everyone, the Crisco Kitchens have developed a number of quick variations with peanut butter as the star. Try Crunchy & Chippy Peanut Butter Cookies and savor the full-bodied peanut flavor. Or pair peanut butter with its traditional partners—chocolate in the dazzling but easy-to-make Inside-Out Peanut Butter Cookie Cups, jelly in kid-pleasing Peanut Butter Thumbprints and bananas in the memorable Bananaramas. In this chapter, peanut butter-flavored cookies are not confined to drop cookies. Use the basic dough to make unbeatable Triple Layer Peanut Butter Bars and no-fuss Peanut Butter & Jelly Streusel Bars.

Discover the versatility of the basic Irresistible Peanut Butter Cookie recipe. Just turn the page and treat the kid in everyone to dynamic peanut butter creations.

Irresistible Peanut Butter Cookies
(page 64)

Irresistible Peanut Butter Cookies

1¼ cups firmly packed light brown sugar
¾ cup creamy peanut butter
½ cup Crisco all-vegetable shortening or ½ Crisco Stick

3 tablespoons milk
1 tablespoon vanilla
1 egg
1¾ cups all-purpose flour
¾ teaspoon baking soda
¾ teaspoon salt

1. Heat oven to 375°F. Place sheets of foil on countertop for cooling cookies.

2. Place brown sugar, peanut butter, shortening, milk and vanilla in large bowl. Beat at medium speed of electric mixer until well blended. Add egg; beat just until blended.

3. Combine flour, baking soda and salt. Add to shortening mixture; beat at low speed just until blended.

4. Drop dough by rounded measuring tablespoonfuls 2 inches apart onto ungreased baking sheet. Flatten dough slightly in crisscross pattern with tines of fork.

5. Bake one baking sheet at a time at 375°F for 7 to 8 minutes or until cookies are set and just beginning to brown. *Do not overbake.* Cool 2 minutes on baking sheet. Remove cookies to foil to cool completely.

Makes about 3 dozen cookies

Inside-Out Peanut Butter Cookie Cups

Cookies

1¼ cups firmly packed light
brown sugar
¾ cup creamy peanut butter
½ cup Crisco all-vegetable
shortening or ½ Crisco
Stick
3 tablespoons milk
1 tablespoon vanilla
1 egg
1¾ cups all-purpose flour
¾ teaspoon baking soda

¾ teaspoon salt

Filling

1 cup (6 ounces) semi-sweet
chocolate chips
1 teaspoon Butter Flavor
Crisco all-vegetable
shortening*
¼ cup finely chopped
peanuts

*Crisco all-vegetable shortening can be substituted for Butter Flavor
Crisco.

1. For cookies, place brown sugar, peanut butter, shortening, milk and
vanilla in large bowl. Beat at medium speed of electric mixer until well
blended. Add egg; beat just until blended.

2. Combine flour, baking soda and salt. Add to shortening mixture;
beat at low speed just until blended. Refrigerate about 1 hour or until
firm.

3. Heat oven to 375°F. Grease mini-muffin pans. Place sheets of foil on
countertop for cooling cookies.

4. Shape dough into 1-inch balls. Place each ball in prepared mini-
muffin cup (1¾ inches in diameter). Press dough onto bottom and
sides of cup to within ½ inch of top.

5. Bake at 375°F for 7 to 8 minutes or until cookies are set and just
beginning to brown. *Do not overbake*. Cool 10 minutes on cooling
racks. Remove cookie cups carefully to foil to cool completely.

6. For filling, place chocolate chips and shortening in medium microwave-
safe bowl. Microwave at 50% (MEDIUM) for 1 to 2 minutes or until
chips are shiny and soft. Stir until smooth. Spoon about ½ teaspoon
chocolate mixture into center of each cookie. Sprinkle with chopped
peanuts. Cool completely.   *Makes about 3½ dozen cookie cups*

Bananaramas

1¼ cups firmly packed light
    brown sugar
¾ cup creamy peanut butter
½ cup Crisco all-vegetable
    shortening or ½ Crisco
    Stick
1 cup mashed banana
3 tablespoons milk
1½ teaspoons vanilla
½ teaspoon almond extract

1 egg
2 cups all-purpose flour
¾ teaspoon baking soda
¾ teaspoon salt
1½ cups milk chocolate
    chunks or semisweet
    chocolate chunks*
1 cup peanuts or coarsely
    chopped pecans
    (optional)

* A combination of milk chocolate and semisweet chocolate chunks can be used.

1. Heat oven to 350°F. Place sheets of foil on countertop for cooling cookies.

2. Place brown sugar, peanut butter, shortening, banana, milk, vanilla and almond extract in large bowl. Beat at medium speed of electric mixer until well blended. Add egg; beat just until blended.

3. Combine flour, baking soda and salt. Add to shortening mixture; beat at low speed just until blended. Stir in chocolate chunks and nuts, if desired.

4. Drop dough by rounded measuring tablespoonfuls 2 inches apart onto ungreased baking sheets.

5. Bake one baking sheet at a time at 350°F for 11 to 13 minutes or until cookies are light brown around edges. *Do not overbake.* Cool 2 minutes on baking sheet. Remove cookies to foil to cool completely.

Makes about 4 dozen cookies

Top to bottom: Bananaramas,
Inside-Out Peanut Butter
Cookie Cups (page 65)

Triple Layer Peanut Butter Bars

Base

1¼ cups firmly packed light
    brown sugar
¾ cup creamy peanut butter
½ cup Crisco all-vegetable
    shortening or ½ Crisco
    Stick
3 tablespoons milk
1 tablespoon vanilla
1 egg
1¾ cups all-purpose flour
¾ teaspoon baking soda
¾ teaspoon salt

Peanut Butter Layer

1½ cups confectioners sugar

2 tablespoons creamy
    peanut butter
1 tablespoon Butter Flavor
    Crisco all-vegetable
    shortening
3 tablespoons milk

Chocolate Glaze

2 squares (1 ounce *each*)
    unsweetened baking
    chocolate
2 tablespoons Butter Flavor
    Crisco all-vegetable
    shortening

1. Heat oven to 350°F. Grease 9 × 13-inch baking pan. Place cooling rack on countertop.

2. For base, place brown sugar, peanut butter, shortening, milk and vanilla in large bowl. Beat at medium speed of electric mixer until well blended. Add egg; beat just until blended.

3. Combine flour, baking soda and salt. Add to shortening mixture; beat at low speed just until blended.

4. Press mixture evenly onto bottom of prepared pan.

5. Bake at 350°F for 18 to 20 minutes or until wooden pick inserted in center comes out clean. *Do not overbake.* Cool completely on cooling rack.

6. For peanut butter layer, place confectioners sugar, peanut butter, shortening and milk in medium bowl. Beat at low speed of electric mixer until smooth. Spread over base. Refrigerate 30 minutes.

7. For chocolate glaze, place chocolate and shortening in small microwave-safe bowl. Microwave at 50% (MEDIUM) for 1 to 2 minutes or until shiny and soft. Stir until smooth. Cool slightly. Spread over peanut butter layer. Refrigerate about 1 hour or until glaze is set. Cut into 3 × 1½-inch bars. Let stand 15 to 20 minutes at room temperature before serving.   *Makes about 2 dozen bars*

Triple Layer Peanut Butter Bars

Peanut Butter & Jelly Streusel Bars

1¼ cups firmly packed light brown
    sugar
¾ cup creamy peanut butter
½ cup Crisco all-vegetable shortening
    or ½ Crisco Stick
3 tablespoons milk
1 tablespoon vanilla
1 egg
1¾ cups all-purpose flour
¾ teaspoon baking soda
¾ teaspoon salt
1 cup strawberry jam, stirred
½ cup quick oats, uncooked

1. Heat oven to 350°F. Grease 13 × 9-inch baking pan. Place cooling rack on countertop.

2. Place brown sugar, peanut butter, shortening, milk and vanilla in large bowl. Beat at medium speed of electric mixer until well blended. Add egg; beat just until blended.

3. Combine flour, baking soda and salt. Add to shortening mixture; beat at low speed just until blended.

4. Press ⅔ of dough onto bottom of prepared baking pan. Spread jam over dough to within ¼ inch of edges.

5. Add oats to remaining dough. Drop dough by spoonfuls onto jam.

6. Bake at 350°F for 20 to 25 minutes or until edges and streusel topping are lightly browned. *Do not overbake.* Cool completely on cooling rack. Cut into 2 × 1½-inch bars.
Makes 3 dozen bars

Clockwise from top left: Peanut Butter & Jelly Streusel Bars, Irresistible Peanut Butter Jack O' Lanterns (page 73), Peanut Butter Sombreros (page 72)

Plan a fun-filled Halloween party— it's easy to do and popular with any age group. For entertainment choose from a seemingly endless list of games—from silly to goulish. Cookies are a perfect fit for your menu because they are quick to prepare and easy to serve. While everyone will love these Peanut Butter & Jelly Streusel Bars, most any cookies will be a hit.

Peanut Butter Sombreros

For even browning, place only one baking sheet at a time in the oven. If the oven does not heat evenly, turn the baking sheet halfway through baking time. Baking sheets can be reused for a second batch of cookies. Just be sure baking sheets have cooled to room temperature before using; otherwise, cookies will spread too much.

1¼ cups firmly packed light brown sugar
¾ cup creamy peanut butter
½ cup Crisco all-vegetable shortening or ½ Crisco Stick
3 tablespoons milk
1 tablespoon vanilla
1 egg
1¾ cups all-purpose flour
¾ teaspoon baking soda
¾ teaspoon salt
Granulated sugar
40 to 50 chocolate kisses, unwrapped

1. Heat oven to 375°F. Place sheets of foil on countertop for cooling cookies.

2. Place brown sugar, peanut butter, shortening, milk and vanilla in large bowl. Beat at medium speed of electric mixer until well blended. Add egg; beat just until blended.

3. Combine flour, baking soda and salt. Add to shortening mixture; beat at low speed just until blended.

4. Shape dough into 1-inch balls. Roll in granulated sugar. Place 2 inches apart on ungreased baking sheets.

5. Bake one baking sheet at a time at 375°F for 6 minutes. Press chocolate kiss into center of each cookie. Bake 3 minutes longer. *Do not overbake.* Cool 2 minutes on baking sheet. Remove cookies to foil to cool completely.   *Makes about 4 dozen cookies*

Irresistible Peanut Butter Jack O' Lanterns

Cookies

1¼ cups firmly packed light brown sugar

¾ cup creamy peanut butter

½ cup Crisco all-vegetable shortening or ½ Crisco Stick

3 tablespoons milk

1 tablespoon vanilla

1 egg

1¾ cups all-purpose flour

¾ teaspoon baking soda

¾ teaspoon salt

Icing

1 cup (6 ounces) semisweet chocolate chips

2 teaspoons Butter Flavor Crisco all-vegetable shortening*

*Crisco all-vegetable shortening can be substituted for Butter Flavor Crisco.

1. Heat oven to 375°F. Place sheets of foil on countertop for cooling cookies.

2. For cookies, place brown sugar, peanut butter, shortening, milk and vanilla in large bowl. Beat at medium speed of electric mixer until well blended. Add egg; beat just until blended.

3. Combine flour, baking soda and salt. Add to shortening mixture; beat at low speed just until blended.

4. Pinch off pieces of dough the size of walnuts. Shape into balls. Place 3 inches apart on ungreased baking sheet. Flatten each ball with bottom of glass to approximately ⅜-inch thickness. Form into pumpkin shape, making indentation on top of round. Pinch off very small piece of dough and roll to form small stem. Attach to top of cookie. Score dough with vertical lines with small, sharp knife to resemble pumpkin.

5. Bake one baking sheet at a time at 375°F for 7 to 8 minutes or until cookies are set and just beginning to brown. *Do not overbake.* Cool on baking sheet 2 minutes. Remove cookies to foil to cool completely.

6. For icing, place chocolate chips and shortening in heavy resealable sandwich bag; seal bag. Microwave at 50% (MEDIUM) for 1 minute. Knead bag. If necessary, microwave at 50% for another 30 seconds at a time until mixture is smooth when bag is kneaded. Cut small tip off corner of bag. Pipe lines and faces on cookies to resemble jack o' lanterns. *Makes about 3 dozen cookies*

Peanut Butter Thumbprints

Peanut butter and jelly seem to have a natural affinity. Kids never outgrow their fondness for this combination, so include these Peanut Butter Thumbprints and Peanut Butter & Jelly Streusel Bars on page 71 in their school lunches or after-school snacks.

1¼ cups firmly packed light brown
    sugar
¾ cup creamy peanut butter
½ cup Crisco all-vegetable shortening
    or ½ Crisco Stick
3 tablespoons milk
1 tablespoon vanilla
1 egg
1¾ cups all-purpose flour
¾ teaspoon baking soda
¾ teaspoon salt
    Granulated sugar
¼ cup strawberry jam,* stirred

*Substitute your favorite jam or jelly for strawberry jam.

1. Heat oven to 375°F. Place sheets of foil on countertop for cooling cookies.

2. Place brown sugar, peanut butter, shortening, milk and vanilla in large bowl. Beat at medium speed of electric mixer until well blended. Add egg; beat just until blended.

3. Combine flour, baking soda and salt. Add to shortening mixture; beat at low speed just until blended.

4. Shape dough into 1-inch balls. Roll in granulated sugar. Place 2 inches apart on ungreased baking sheets.

5. Bake one baking sheet at a time at 375°F for 6 minutes. Press centers of cookies immediately with back of measuring teaspoon. Bake 3 minutes longer or until cookies are set and just beginning to brown. *Do not overbake.* Cool 2 minutes on baking sheet. Spoon jam into center of each cookie. Remove cookies to foil to cool completely.
Makes about 4 dozen cookies

Peanut Butter Thumbprints

Crunchy & Chippy Peanut Butter Cookies

1¼ cups firmly packed light
  brown sugar
¾ cup crunchy peanut
  butter
½ cup Crisco all-vegetable
  shortening or ½ Crisco
  Stick
3 tablespoons milk
1 tablespoon vanilla

1 egg
1¾ cups all-purpose flour
¾ teaspoon baking soda
¾ teaspoon salt
1 cup (6 ounces) miniature
  semisweet chocolate
  chips
1 cup chopped peanuts*

*Salted, unsalted or dry roasted peanuts can be used.

1. Heat oven to 375°F. Place sheets of foil on countertop for cooling cookies.

2. Place brown sugar, peanut butter, shortening, milk and vanilla in large bowl. Beat at medium speed of electric mixer until well blended. Add egg; beat just until blended.

3. Combine flour, baking soda and salt. Add to shortening mixture; beat at low speed just until blended. Stir in small chocolate chips and peanuts.

4. Drop dough by rounded measuring tablespoonfuls 2 inches apart onto ungreased baking sheets. Flatten slightly with fingers.

5. Bake one baking sheet at a time at 375°F for 7 to 8 minutes or until cookies are set and just beginning to brown. *Do not overbake.* Cool 2 minutes on baking sheet. Remove cookies to foil to cool completely.

Makes about 3 dozen cookies

*Top to bottom: Crunchy & Chippy
Peanut Butter Cookies, Almond
Mocha Cookie Bars (page 85)*

CHEWY BROWNIE COOKIES

For a true chocolate lover, nothing compares with the rich chocolaty flavor of a brownie. And now that flavor has been captured in the Chewy Brownie Cookie, a luscious drop cookie with a double dose of chocolate. This cookie, developed by the Crisco Kitchens to be moist and chewy, is sure to please any chocoholic on your guest list.

Some of the variations in this chapter are drawn from time-honored, crowd-pleasing chocolate flavor combinations. Chocolate-Mint Brownie Cookies team two old favorites. Friends will love the richness of Caramel Nut Chocolate Cookies and fruity Double Chocolate Cherry Cookies inspired by the old-world flavor of Black Forest cake. Chocolate is a natural with coffee and almonds in Almond Mocha Cookie Bars. Or, press this basic chewy brownie dough into a baking pan and top with a cream cheese layer for heavenly Chocolate Cheesecake Bars.

Chocolate cookies are always welcome at any holiday celebration or special occasion. Explore this dark and fudgy collection of brownie cookie variations today. You will find inspiration at every turn.

Chewy Brownie Cookies (page 80)

Chewy Brownie Cookies

1½ cups firmly packed light
   brown sugar
⅔ cup Crisco all-vegetable
   shortening or ⅔ Crisco
   Stick
1 tablespoon water
1 teaspoon vanilla
2 eggs

1½ cups all-purpose flour
⅓ cup unsweetened cocoa
   powder
½ teaspoon salt
¼ teaspoon baking soda
2 cups (12 ounces)
   semisweet chocolate
   chips

1. Heat oven to 375°F. Place sheets of foil on countertop for cooling cookies.

2. Place brown sugar, shortening, water and vanilla in large bowl. Beat at medium speed of electric mixer until well blended. Add eggs; beat well.

3. Combine flour, cocoa, salt and baking soda. Add to shortening mixture; beat at low speed just until blended. Stir in chocolate chips.

4. Drop dough by rounded measuring tablespoonfuls 2 inches apart onto ungreased baking sheet.

5. Bake one baking sheet at a time at 375°F for 7 to 9 minutes or until cookies are set. *Do not overbake.* Cool 2 minutes on baking sheet. Remove cookies to foil to cool completely.

Makes about 3 dozen cookies

Toasted Almond Brownie Cookies

1 cup blanched whole almonds
1½ cups firmly packed light brown sugar
⅔ cup Crisco all-vegetable shortening or ⅔ Crisco Stick
1 tablespoon water
1 teaspoon almond extract
2 eggs
1½ cups all-purpose flour
⅓ cup unsweetened cocoa powder
½ teaspoon salt
¼ teaspoon baking soda
2 cups (12 ounces) semisweet chocolate chips

1. Heat oven to 350°F. Spread almonds on baking sheet; bake at 350°F for 7 to 10 minutes or until golden brown, stirring several times. Cool. Chop coarsely; reserve.

2. *Increase oven temperature to 375°F.* Place sheets of foil on countertop for cooling cookies.

3. Place brown sugar, shortening, water and almond extract in large bowl. Beat at medium speed of electric mixer until well blended. Add eggs; beat well.

4. Combine flour, cocoa, salt and baking soda. Add to shortening mixture; beat at low speed just until blended. Stir in chocolate chips and reserved almonds.

5. Drop dough by rounded measuring tablespoonfuls 2 inches apart onto ungreased baking sheet.

6. Bake one baking sheet at a time at 375°F for 7 to 9 minutes or until cookies are set. *Do not overbake.* Cool 2 minutes on baking sheet. Remove cookies to foil to cool completely. *Makes about 3 dozen cookies*

Plan ahead! To have freshly baked cookies ready in minutes, place dough in a tightly covered container and refrigerate up to one week or freeze up to six months. Or, form cookies on baking sheet, freeze and transfer to plastic bag for up to six months. Thaw dough before baking.

Double Chocolate Cherry Cookies

Cookies

- 1½ cups firmly packed light brown sugar
- ⅔ cup Crisco all-vegetable shortening or ⅔ Crisco Stick
- 1 tablespoon water
- 1 teaspoon vanilla
- 2 eggs
- 1½ cups all-purpose flour
- ⅓ cup unsweetened cocoa powder
- ½ teaspoon salt
- ¼ teaspoon baking soda
- 30 to 40 maraschino cherries

Icing

- ½ cup semisweet chocolate chips or white chocolate chips
- ½ teaspoon Crisco all-vegetable shortening

1. Heat oven to 375°F. Place sheets of foil on countertop for cooling cookies.

2. For cookies, place brown sugar, shortening, water and vanilla in large bowl. Beat at medium speed of electric mixer until well blended. Add eggs; beat well.

3. Combine flour, cocoa, salt and baking soda. Add to shortening mixture; beat at low speed just until blended.

4. Shape rounded measuring tablespoonful of dough around each maraschino cherry, covering cherry completely. Place cookies 2 inches apart on ungreased baking sheet.

5. Bake one baking sheet at a time at 375°F for 7 to 9 minutes or until cookies are set. *Do not overbake*. Cool 2 minutes on baking sheet. Remove cookies to foil to cool completely.

6. For icing, place chocolate chips and shortening in heavy resealable sandwich bag; seal bag. Microwave at 50% (MEDIUM) for 1 minute. Knead bag. If necessary, microwave at 50% another 30 seconds at a time until mixture is smooth when bag is kneaded. Cut small tip off corner of bag; drizzle chocolate over cookies.

Makes about 3 dozen cookies

Double Chocolate Cherry Cookies

Chocolate Cheesecake Bars

Brownies

1½ cups firmly packed light brown sugar

⅔ cup Crisco all-vegetable shortening or ⅔ Crisco Stick

1 tablespoon water

1 teaspoon vanilla

2 eggs

1½ cups all-purpose flour

⅓ cup unsweetened cocoa powder

½ teaspoon salt

¼ teaspoon baking soda

2 cups (12 ounces) miniature semisweet chocolate chips

Topping

1 (8-ounce) *plus* 1 (3-ounce) package cream cheese, softened

2 eggs

¾ cup granulated sugar

1 teaspoon vanilla

1. Heat oven to 350°F. Grease 13 × 9-inch baking pan. Place cooling rack on countertop.

2. For brownies, place brown sugar, shortening, water and vanilla in large bowl. Beat at medium speed of electric mixer until well blended. Add eggs; beat well.

3. Combine flour, cocoa, salt and baking soda. Add to shortening mixture; beat at low speed just until blended. Stir in small chocolate chips. Spread dough evenly onto bottom of prepared pan.

4. For topping, place cream cheese, eggs, granulated sugar and vanilla in medium bowl. Beat at medium speed until well blended. Spread evenly over top of brownie mixture.

5. Bake at 350°F for 35 to 40 minutes or until set. *Do not overbake.* Place on cooling rack. Run spatula around edge of pan to loosen. Cool completely on cooling rack. Cut into 2 × 1½-inch bars. Garnish as desired. *Makes about 3 dozen brownies*

Almond Mocha Cookie Bars

Cookie Base

1 cup slivered almonds
1½ cups firmly packed light
   brown sugar
⅔ cup Crisco all-vegetable
   shortening or ⅔ Crisco
   Stick
2 tablespoons instant or
   espresso coffee powder
1 tablespoon cold coffee
1 teaspoon vanilla
½ teaspoon almond extract
2 eggs
1½ cups all-purpose flour
⅓ cup unsweetened cocoa
   powder

½ teaspoon salt
¼ teaspoon baking soda
1 cup (6 ounces) miniature
   semisweet chocolate
   chips

Glaze

1 cup confectioners sugar
1 tablespoon cold coffee
1 tablespoon coffee-flavored
   liqueur or cold coffee
   (optional)

1. Heat oven to 350°F. Grease 13 × 9-inch baking pan. Place cooling rack on countertop.

2. For cookie base, spread almonds on baking sheet; bake at 350°F for 7 to 10 minutes or until golden brown, stirring several times. Cool completely. Chop coarsely.

3. Place brown sugar, shortening, coffee powder, coffee, vanilla and almond extract in large bowl. Beat at medium speed of electric mixer until well blended. Add eggs; beat well.

4. Combine flour, cocoa, salt and baking soda. Add to shortening mixture; beat at low speed just until blended. Stir in small chocolate chips and reserved almonds. Spread mixture evenly into prepared pan.

5. Bake at 350°F for 30 to 35 minutes or until set. *Do not overbake.* Cool completely on wire rack. Cut into 2 × 1½-inch bars.

6. For glaze, combine confectioners sugar, coffee and coffee liqueur, if desired, in small bowl. Stir until well blended. Add additional coffee, a little at a time, if icing is too thick, or add additional confectioners sugar, if icing is too thin. Drizzle glaze over bars.

Makes about 3 dozen bars

German Chocolate Brownie Cookies

Cookies
- 1½ cups firmly packed light brown sugar
- ⅔ cup Crisco all-vegetable shortening or ⅔ Crisco Stick
- 1 tablespoon water
- 1 teaspoon vanilla
- 2 eggs
- 1½ cups all-purpose flour
- ⅓ cup unsweetened cocoa powder
- ½ teaspoon salt
- ¼ teaspoon baking soda
- 2 cups (12 ounces) semisweet chocolate chips

Topping
- ½ cup evaporated milk
- ½ cup granulated sugar
- ¼ cup Butter Flavor Crisco all-vegetable shortening or ¼ Butter Flavor Crisco Stick*
- 2 egg yolks, lightly beaten
- ½ teaspoon vanilla
- ½ cup chopped pecans
- ½ cup flaked coconut

*Crisco all-vegetable shortening can be substituted for Butter Flavor Crisco or Butter Flavor Crisco Stick.

1. Heat oven to 375°F. Place sheets of foil on countertop for cooling cookies.

2. For cookies, place brown sugar, shortening, water and vanilla in large bowl. Beat at medium speed of electric mixer until well blended. Add eggs; beat well.

3. Combine flour, cocoa, salt and baking soda. Add to shortening mixture; beat at low speed just until blended. Stir in chocolate chips.

4. Drop dough by rounded measuring tablespoonfuls 2 inches apart onto ungreased baking sheet.

5. Bake one baking sheet at a time at 375°F for 7 to 9 minutes or until cookies are set. *Do not overbake.* Cool 2 minutes on baking sheet. Remove cookies to foil to cool completely.

6. For topping, combine evaporated milk, granulated sugar, shortening and egg yolks in medium saucepan. Stir over medium heat until thickened. Remove from heat. Stir in vanilla, pecans and coconut. Cool completely. Frost cookies. *Makes about 3 dozen cookies*

Top to bottom: Maple Pecan Sandwich Cookies (page 56), German Chocolate Brownie Cookies, Good 'n' Tasties (page 37)

Caramel Nut Chocolate Cookies

1½ cups firmly packed light
    brown sugar
⅔ cup Crisco all-vegetable
    shortening or ⅔ Crisco
    Stick
1 tablespoon water
1 teaspoon vanilla
2 eggs
1¾ cups all-purpose flour
⅓ cup unsweetened cocoa
    powder

½ teaspoon salt
¼ teaspoon baking soda
2 cups (12 ounces)
    miniature semisweet
    chocolate chips
1 cup chopped pecans
20 to 25 caramels,
    unwrapped and halved

1. Heat oven to 375°F. Place sheets of foil on countertop for cooling cookies.

2. Place brown sugar, shortening, water and vanilla in large bowl. Beat at medium speed of electric mixer until well blended. Add eggs; beat well.

3. Combine flour, cocoa, salt and baking soda. Add to shortening mixture; beat at low speed just until blended. Stir in small chocolate chips.

4. Shape dough into 1¼-inch balls. Dip tops in chopped pecans. Place 2 inches apart on ungreased baking sheet. Press caramel half in center of each ball.

5. Bake one baking sheet at a time at 375°F for 7 to 9 minutes or until cookies are set. *Do not overbake.* Cool 2 minutes on baking sheet. Remove cookies to foil to cool completely.

Makes about 4 dozen cookies

Caramel Nut Chocolate Cookies

Cracked Chocolate Cookies

1½ cups firmly packed light brown sugar
⅔ cup Crisco all-vegetable shortening or ⅔ Crisco Stick
1 tablespoon water
1 teaspoon vanilla
2 eggs
1½ cups all-purpose flour

⅓ cup unsweetened cocoa powder
½ teaspoon salt
¼ teaspoon baking soda
2 cups (12 ounces) miniature semisweet chocolate chips
1 cup confectioners sugar

1. Heat oven to 375°F. Place sheets of foil on countertop for cooling cookies.

2. Place brown sugar, shortening, water and vanilla in large bowl. Beat at medium speed of electric mixer until well blended. Add eggs; beat well.

3. Combine flour, cocoa, salt and baking soda. Add to shortening mixture; beat at low speed just until blended. Stir in small chocolate chips.

4. Shape dough into 1¼-inch balls. Roll in confectioners sugar. Place 2 inches apart on ungreased baking sheet.

5. Bake one baking sheet at a time at 375°F for 7 to 9 minutes or until cookies are set. *Do not overbake.* Cool 2 minutes on baking sheet. Remove cookies to foil to cool completely.

Makes about 4 dozen cookies

Chocolate Malted Cookies

¾ cup firmly packed light brown sugar
⅔ cup Crisco all-vegetable shortening or ⅔ Crisco Stick
1 teaspoon vanilla
1 egg
1¾ cups all-purpose flour

½ cup malted milk powder
⅓ cup unsweetened cocoa powder
¾ teaspoon baking soda
½ teaspoon salt
2 cups malted milk balls, broken into large pieces*

*Place malted milk balls in heavy resealable plastic bag; break malted milk balls with rolling pin or back of heavy spoon.

1. Heat oven to 375°F. Place sheets of foil on countertop for cooling cookies.

2. Place brown sugar, shortening and vanilla in large bowl. Beat at medium speed of electric mixer until well blended. Add egg; beat well.

3. Combine flour, malted milk powder, cocoa, baking soda and salt. Add to shortening mixture; beat at low speed just until blended. Stir in malted milk pieces.

4. Drop dough by rounded measuring tablespoonfuls 2 inches apart onto ungreased baking sheet.

5. Bake one baking sheet at a time at 375°F for 7 to 9 minutes or until cookies are set. *Do not overbake.* Cool 2 minutes on baking sheet. Remove cookies to foil to cool completely.

Makes about 3 dozen cookies

Chocolate-Mint Brownie Cookies

1½ cups firmly packed light brown sugar
⅔ cup Crisco all-vegetable shortening or ⅔ Crisco Stick
1 tablespoon water
1 teaspoon vanilla
½ teaspoon peppermint extract

2 eggs
1½ cups all-purpose flour
⅓ cup unsweetened cocoa powder
½ teaspoon salt
¼ teaspoon baking soda
2 cups (12 ounces) mint chocolate chips

1. Heat oven to 375°F. Place sheets of foil on countertop for cooling cookies.

2. Place brown sugar, shortening, water, vanilla and peppermint extract in large bowl. Beat at medium speed of electric mixer until well blended. Add eggs; beat well.

3. Combine flour, cocoa, salt and baking soda. Add to shortening mixture; beat at low speed just until blended. Stir in mint chocolate chips.

4. Drop dough by rounded measuring tablespoonfuls 2 inches apart onto ungreased baking sheet.

5. Bake one baking sheet at a time at 375°F for 7 to 9 minutes or until cookies are set. *Do not overbake.* Cool 2 minutes on baking sheet. Remove cookies to foil to cool completely.

Makes about 3 dozen cookies

White Chocolate Chunk & Macadamia Nut Brownie Cookies

1½ cups firmly packed light brown sugar
⅔ cup Crisco all-vegetable shortening or ⅔ Crisco Stick
1 tablespoon water
1 teaspoon vanilla
2 eggs
1½ cups all-purpose flour
⅓ cup unsweetened cocoa powder
½ teaspoon salt
¼ teaspoon baking soda
1 cup white chocolate chunks or chips
1 cup coarsely chopped macadamia nuts

1. Heat oven to 375°F. Place sheets of foil on countertop for cooling cookies.

2. Place brown sugar, shortening, water and vanilla in large bowl. Beat at medium speed of electric mixer until well blended. Add eggs; beat well.

3. Combine flour, cocoa, salt and baking soda. Add to shortening mixture; beat at low speed just until blended. Stir in white chocolate chunks and macadamia nuts.

4. Drop dough by rounded measuring tablespoonfuls 2 inches apart onto ungreased baking sheet.

5. Bake one baking sheet at a time at 375°F for 7 to 9 minutes or until cookies are set. *Do not overbake.* Cool 2 minutes on baking sheet. Remove cookies to foil to cool completely.

Makes about 3 dozen cookies

White Chocolate Chunk & Macadamia Nut Brownie Cookies

INDEX

METRIC CONVERSION CHART

VOLUME MEASUREMENTS (dry)

⅛ teaspoon = 0.5 mL

¼ teaspoon = 1 mL

½ teaspoon = 2 mL

¾ teaspoon = 4 mL

1 teaspoon = 5 mL

1 tablespoon = 15 mL

2 tablespoons = 30 mL

¼ cup = 60 mL

⅓ cup = 75 mL

½ cup = 125 mL

⅔ cup = 150 mL

¾ cup = 175 mL

1 cup = 250 mL

2 cups = 1 pint = 500 mL

3 cups = 750 mL

4 cups = 1 quart = 1 L

VOLUME MEASUREMENTS (fluid)

1 fluid ounce (2 tablespoons) = 30 mL

4 fluid ounces (½ cup) = 125 mL

8 fluid ounces (1 cup) = 250 mL

12 fluid ounces (1½ cups) = 375 mL

16 fluid ounces (2 cups) = 500 mL

WEIGHTS (mass)

½ ounce = 15 g

1 ounce = 30 g

3 ounces = 90 g

4 ounces = 120 g

8 ounces = 225 g

10 ounces = 285 g

12 ounces = 360 g

16 ounces = 1 pound = 450 g

DIMENSIONS

1/16 inch = 2 mm

⅛ inch = 3 mm

¼ inch = 6 mm

½ inch = 1.5 cm

¾ inch = 2 cm

1 inch = 2.5 cm

OVEN TEMPERATURES

250°F = 120°C

275°F = 140°C

300°F = 150°C

325°F = 160°C

350°F = 180°C

375°F = 190°C

400°F = 200°C

425°F = 220°C

450°F = 230°C

BAKING PAN SIZES

Utensil	Size in Inches/ Quarts	Metric Volume	Size in Centimeters
Baking or Cake Pan (square or rectangular)	8 × 8 × 2	2 L	20 × 20 × 5
	9 × 9 × 2	2.5 L	22 × 22 × 5
	12 × 8 × 2	3 L	30 × 20 × 5
	13 × 9 × 2	3.5 L	33 × 23 × 5
Loaf Pan	8 × 4 × 3	1.5 L	20 × 10 × 7
	9 × 5 × 3	2 L	23 × 13 × 7
Round Layer Cake Pan	8 × 1½	1.2 L	20 × 4
	9 × 1½	1.5 L	23 × 4
Pie Plate	8 × 1¼	750 mL	20 × 3
	9 × 1¼	1 L	23 × 3
Baking Dish or Casserole	1 quart	1 L	—
	1½ quart	1.5 L	—
	2 quart	2 L	—